Caribbean Mythology and Modern Life
Second Edition

Dr. Paloma Mohamed was born in Georgetown, Guyana. She was educated at the University of Guyana, Harvard University and the University of the West Indies. She is a prizewinning poet, essayist, playwright and director. She teaches research, broadcasting and social psychology at the University of Guyana. She was recently named first female Caribbean Laureate of Excellence in Arts and Letters (2015) by the Sabga Foundation.

Caribbean Mythology and Modern Life
5 Plays for Young People

Written by Paloma Mohamed
Illustrations by Barrington Braithwaithe
Preface by Efebo Wilkinson
Introduction by Al Creighton

Designed by: Paloma Mohamed & Harris Art Productions
Cover Design and Illustrations: Barrington Braithwaithe
Introduction by Al Creighton
Preface by Efebo Wilkinson

To my son Shabaka
and to the young people of the Caribbean:

know that you stand upon the shoulders of great ones,
therefore you are taller than you believe.

And to the memories of these great dramatists of the Caribbean:
Sheik Sadiq, Norman Cameron, Errol Hill, Andre Sobryan,
Frank Pilgrim, Laxmie Khalicharran and Robert Narain.

Table of Contents

Foreword
  Carmen Jarvis -I
Remarks
  Desiree Whyles-Ogle -ii
Acknowledgments – *iii*
Preface
  Efebo Wilkinson
Introduction
  Al Creighton –iv
List of Illustrations: - *xxv*
Notes on Set Design and Staging of these plays
1. Chupacabra - 11 -55
    Chupacabra Glossary and notes
2. The Massacuraman -56-82
    The Massacuraman Glossary and notes
3. Sukanti - 83- 109
    Sukanti glossary and notes
4. Anansi's Way -110-152
    Anansi's Way Glossary and notes
5. The Fair Maids Tale - 153- 161
    A Fairmaids Tale Glossary and notes
6. Further Reading

FOREWORD
Carmen Jarvis, UNESCO

UNESCO has always recognized the importance of literature in exploring and understanding life. To this end, the organization has been in the forefront of preserving and fostering culture and education. *Caribbean Mythology and Modern Life*, encompasses many elements with which we are concerned. The book links folk characters and mythology,(fast becoming lost), with particular and universal modern concerns of young people in Guyana, the Caribbean and perhaps the wider world. There are lessons to be learnt from the ordinary folk, even today.

Caribbean Mythology and Modern Life, represents several years of hard work by notable persons in the field of literature, drama, design, education and research, both inside and outside of Guyana. We thank them for their labors. We know it was mostly out of love that this project was completed. Special thanks also to The Majority Press, Inc for supporting the printing of this book.

The publication is a contribution to the youth of Guyana in the promotion of love of drama. I hope that it may in some way help to point the way forward in this area of culture. May our young people get to know and create a better world.

Mrs. Carmen Jarvis
UNESCO
Georgetown, Guyana
July, 2003

REMARKS

Desiree Whyles- Ogle
Unit of Allied Arts, Ministry of Education (Guyana)

A program for Drama in schools is a worthwhile investment since Drama provides an opportunity for students to develop their skills of reading, writing ,speaking and listening among other benefits.

As the old Chinese Proverb denotes

> I hear and I forget,
> I listen and I remember,
> I do and I understand.

This book of plays provides valuable information germane to Guyanese folklore and will serve as a stimulus for Drama productions in schools.

The Allied Arts Unit of the Ministry of Education in Guyana ,wishes to express sincere gratitude to Ms Paloma Mohamed for her continuous support in the promotion of Drama in Education. We also wish to thank Mrs. Carmen Jarvis, UNESCO, The Majority Press Inc., and all those others who have helped to make this book possible.

Best wishes
Desiree Wyles – Ogle,
Administrator Allied Arts Unit - Ministry of Education

ACKNOWLEDGEMENTS

I am particularly pleased to finally present plays specifically written for young people. I am also happy that I was given the opportunity to do this now, when I am so very sensitive to the particular cultural treasures of the Caribbean and when so many things threaten to erode that culture and destroy our young people and our societies. These plays try to address some of these issues.

There are so many people to thank. Desiree Whyles and the staff at Allied Arts in Georgetown, Guyana pressed me into service again and again, thereby forcing me into contact with teachers and students. UNICEF my employer at the time, allowed me to support Allied Arts. In the process, we found that drama lent itself very well to education and the ventilation of sensitive issues. However, there was no such material readily available. Carmen Jarvis and UNESCO then contributed financial resources to develop the plays in this book, which I believe is the first at least in Guyana if not the Caribbean. The Ministry of Education gave its full support. Still, lacking the full resources to produce a top of the line book, I pressed my friends into service; Efebo Wilkinson as primary dramaturge but also to write the notes on theatre for children and young people; Al Creighton of the University of Guyana to provide a solid introduction; Barrington Braithwaite, artist and folklorists to research and illustrate the folk characters; Harris Art to design the book and most importantly The Majority Press to foot the costs of printing and supplying free copies to Guyanese schools. So you see this was really a co-operative effort. I totally appreciate the commitment and contributions of these rare and gifted people.

My personal thanks also to these talented actors and actresses who dramaturged the plays:

In Guyana: Francis Pearce, Gem Mahadoo, Mignon Lowe, Cicley Forbes, Beverly Hinds, Jennifer Thomas, George Braithwaithe, Ansford Patrick, Wynette Oudkirk, Nora (?), Imitaz Panday, Samantha Panday ;

In Trinidad at the Center for Creative and Festival Arts : Kentillia Louis, Alicia Goddard, Ebony Roach, Arthea Octore, Seone Viacva, Darin Gibson, Foti George, Leekeesha Pincarin, Victor Edwards, Onika Henry, Kevin McMayo, Davlin Thomas, Samantha Pierre, Eric Barry, Damian Richardson.

Apart from those directly involved in the production of the book, I feel compelled to thank these others for their continued support, guidance and wisdom which they have always shared abundantly with me: Special thanks to my husband Tony, Alwin Bully, Victor Edwards, Norvan Fullerton, Daphne Rogers, Denyse Gomes, Mel and Cecil Bovell, Zena Lashly, Charles Hinds, Herbie Harper, Zeno Constance, Vic Insanally, Roopnandan Singh, Kit Nascimento, Bill Pilgrim, Ken Danns, Anande Trotman, Atta Britton, Dorothy, Caroline , Jacqueline and Sandra Smartt and mother Marie Mohamed and my brothers Ramon, Raymond and Raoul. I must also thank Pearl Eintou Springer, the only other female Caribbean playwright that I know, for her example of courage and cultural rigor. I know there are many others whose love and prayers are always with me. I thank you and I thank God for continued grace and light upon my life.

Paloma
Port of Spain, Trinidad
October, 2003.

PREFACE

THEATRE FOR CHILDREN AND YOUNG PEOPLE: CAPTURING THE GENIUS OF THE GRIOT

If we hope to live not just from moment to moment, but in true consciousness of our existence, then our greatest need and most difficult achievement is to find meaning in our lives.
Bruno Bettelheim

When Bruno Bettelheim wrote *The Uses of Enchantment* in 1975 he was responding to a growing tendency, at the time, on the part of many educators, psychologists and librarians, among others, to regard the folk/fairy tale as a dangerous form of literature.

There were those who, in those days (regarded by many as a period of a new enlightenment), objected to the tales primarily on the grounds that they contained too many graphic scenes of "violence and gore." Others even went further, according to Jed H. Davis and Mary Jane Evans, in their book *Theatre, Children and Youth* (Anchorage 1982). Some along with the usual objection to violence, took issue with the fact that folk/fairy tales tended generally to concern themselves with "unmentionable subjects": deep-seated, guilt-filled wishes and fears, and worrisome issues not normally given voice by civilized society, and which the child, normally, "dares not discuss with anyone" (74).

But those are precisely two of the reasons why Bettelheim, in his book referred to above, lauded the fairy tale, recommending it as a rich source of enlightenment and entertainment for both children and adults. He described his book as an attempt to demonstrate, not only the ways in which folk/fairy stories represent in a highly imaginative and entertaining form, what "the process of healthy human development consists of," but more importantly, the manner in which the tales make such development appear to the child as an attractive proposition in which to engage (12).

In the folk/fairy tale, he argued, all situations are simplified, with details, unless absolutely essential to the plot, completely eliminated. All characters, no matter how large the cast, are always clearly drawn, representing types rather than being unique. And the problem, the central issues to be addressed (what he refers to as the "existential dilemma"), is always stated so briefly and pointedly as to permit the child to come to grips with it in its most essential form. Nothing, he concluded, from the entire stock of children's literature, with rare exceptions, "can be as enriching and satisfying to child and adult alike as the folk fairy tale" (5).

What Bettelheim, through his long years of patient research, concluded is not fundamentally different from what dramatists who specialize in making theatre for children and young people have always instinctively understood: the need for lean, clean, story-lines and plots that keep such simplicity intact. Of course, "simplicity" by no means suggests "simplistic" or lacking in complexity. And, indeed, children and young people have, time and again, demonstrated their capacity and willingness to handle complex and very involved issues. The concern here is with the clarity and lack of clutter with which each element of the drama is constructed; a clarity that should be present regardless of the creative complexity of theatrical devices employed, the eloquence of language voiced by the different characters or the intricate elegance of design features.

It is to be expected, therefore, that in their search for source material to make appropriate theatre for young audiences, dramatists would look towards the world's stock of folk/fairy tales. Several of the better-known ones have found expression on many of the world's stages in musical and non-musical form, in amateur and professional productions. No doubt there have been more than a few productions of questionable quality, but in the main, folk/fairy tales, when presented in dramatic form, tend to hold the attention of young audiences. Children, in particular, never tire of seeing their favourite fables come alive on stage.

Nellie McCaslin, recognized world-wide for her leadership role and scholarship in Creative Drama as well as in Young People's Theatre, reminds us in her book, *Creative Drama in the Classroom*, that for the playwright to succeed in the theatre, his/her play must contain the twin ingredients of taste and credibility "combined with a worthwhile idea, a hero with whom the audience can identify, action, poetic justice, substance, and literary quality" (155). It is no wonder then to find that she strongly advises that:

> Myths, legends, and folktales are particularly good for creative playing. In the first place, these stories have been told and retold over the years so that the story line is clear and easily followed. Characters are generally well defined; have complete relevance to the plot; and, even in the case of the supernatural, have credibility. The theme is usually strong, for one generation has passed the tale along to the next, carefully, if unconsciously, preserving the values of the culture. (163)

In today's world of cutting-edge technology, high-speed information flows, and virtual images, the Caribbean remains a particularly rich resource area for traditional folk material. In some instances the folk music and folk dances of the Caribbean region have received some degree of popularization worldwide. The music, in particular, has entered the entertainment markets of most Capitals as folk derived popular musical forms: Reggae, Calypso, Cadance and Zouk. The rich stock of Caribbean folktales, myths and legends, however, still remains relatively unknown and untapped. The folktale, in particular, often called the "Nancy Story" is a very prominent feature of the Caribbean culture-scape, known as much for its biting wit and colourful characters, as for the life-lessons that it teaches.

Kenneth Vidia Parmasad, Caribbean Historian, scholar and writer, in his *Salt and Roti: Indian Folk Tales of the Caribbean*, reminds us, not only that the art of story-telling dates back to the very beginning of human culture, but also, that it was the story-teller, the griot, who was "the living store-house of all the history of the tribe," representing the "accumulated experiences" of his people and transmitting, through his stories, "the wisdom of the ancients from one generation to the next" (xiv).

He, like other historians, folklorists and anthropologists working the Caribbean in an earlier period (notably Jacob D. Elder, Andrew Carr, Andrew Pearse, Melville and Frances Herskovits), recognized that in (what he calls) "these transplanted societies" of the Caribbean, made up of principally "displaced peoples and races," many practices were transplanted. Transplantation into the Caribbean was almost wholesale from the former homelands of European settlers, enslaved Africans and indentured labourers brought into the region from India, China and the Middle East as replacement labour to work the sugar-cane plantations when the system of slavery ended in 1834.

According to Parmasad, one such practice among descendants of East Indian indentured labourers, was the tradition of story-telling, which, "in Trinidad was quite popular and quite strong up to the mid-1950's" (xv). Nor was it any different among the other displaced peoples. In homes across the region, or at special gatherings such as birthdays, thanksgivings and "satsangs" (a communal get-together), the raconteur, usually one of the senior women of the clan, would soon enough occupy center-stage and in a practiced voice, engage her spellbound listeners.

And spellbound indeed they always were. For our Caribbean griots never only voiced their parts. They sang; they danced, and crafted a living prose . . . a complete, "cross-vocabulary" theatre. The tone was always right; the movement, captivating. Parmasad completes the picture:

> In the home also, the practice of story-telling was very much a living tradition. On evenings, as the lighted flambeaux danced with shadows on the walls, all the children of the often extended family would gather round the grandmother seated in a hammock and listen with rapt attention to the adventures of the boy Gopala, to the mischief-making of Sakchulee or to any number of animal stories, fables and folk tales. (xvi)

Parmasad was speaking mainly of East Indian families in Trinidad and Tobago, but among the other ethnic groups across the region, the situation was very much the same. The names of the folk characters might have been different (Papa Bois, Masacuraman, Mama Dlo, Ananci) but the impact, the excitement, the enchantment were very much the same.

And from those stories, lessons were learned: life-lessons about heroic deeds and loyalty to family and community and reverence to the Gods and the tremendous healing power of love. Through those stories, community elders gave to floundering youth much needed wise counsel on responsibility, morality, self-discipline, and trust, each child, each young adult seated in the communal circle of the story-teller's reach, participating fully in the unfolding drama, sharing the passion and the triumphs and the pain before walking away at the story's close, that much richer for having lived the particular fictional experience.

That's precisely the "moment" that Paloma Mohamed seeks to capture in each play included in this collection: a gathering of youthful listeners grouped around the familiar griot (the village raconteur), eager faces barely visible in the light of the flickering flambeau, and the tale, so cleanly cut, unfolding in full colour and layered dramatic form before the several up-turned eyes. This is the magic she hopes to create as a means of imparting, through the vehicle of the folk drama, precious lessons about living to the young.

Her story-lines are drawn in simple linear fashion, her characters no less rooted in the folk and certainly no less interesting than those of the traditional village griot. Drawn from the folklore of Guyana, they must have had an earlier non-Caribbean existence (as did Ananci and Sakchulee) before becoming fully Caribbean in look and feel and language and overall sensibilities. In any event, she makes use of a number of folk characters that appear to have taken up residence in more than one Caribbean country including Ol Higue, Ananci himself and the Soucouyant.

Caribbean playwrights, over the years, have drawn on the folk traditions to create works of striking dramatic quality. Among the best known would be Nobel Laureate Derek Walcott's *Ti Jean and his Brothers* and the late Errol Hill's *Dance Bongo*. In addition, two emerging theatrical styles of the Caribbean, The Jamaica Pantomime and The Best Village Theatre of Trinidad and Tobago, make generous, highly creative and effective use of the folk material of the region, but none of this is collected and widely accessible.

Paloma Mohamed's collection of short plays, therefore, that looks to the folk characters, folktales, myths, mysteries and legends of Guyana for source material is a welcome addition to Caribbean dramatic material for young audiences. That they are specifically intended to teach life skills to the young should render them no less interesting, no less entertaining, no less satisfying an experience.

Lester Efebo Wilkinson
Port of Spain
February 13, 2004

Dr. Lester Efebo Wilkinson is a celebrated Trinidadian playwright and poet. He has been an Ambassador, Educator and arts activist for over 50 years. He currently teaches at the Centre for Creative and Festival Arts, University of the West Indies and is a much sought after consultant in the areas of cultural and arts policy.

INTRODUCTION

Since the rise of modern Guyanese drama in the 1940s there have been several local playwrights, but very few who can claim a place as major dramatists of the era. Most of them emerged during a particularly lively period between 1980 and 2000 when, collectively, they contributed to an important development in contemporary Guyanese popular theatre, but very few achieved the stature as a playwright of excellence or significant influence over the state of Guyanese theatre. During the whole period of roughly 60 years there were quite different forces which motivated the dramatists and provided opportunities for production, creating a different type of theatre each time.

This 'modern' period emerged during a particularly prosperous advance of popular theatre around the Caribbean when vaudeville, comedy, calypso tents and shanto entertained large audiences in cinema houses. At that time there were strong connections between Guyana and Trinidad including frequent exchanges of producers and performers. The most significant factor as far as dramatic production is concerned, is that the audiences were largely working class and the stages were provided by cinemas (movie theatres). This was a major shift from the formal theatre dominated by the middle class with more conventional venues like the Theatre Royal and the Assembly Rooms.

Yet, in spite of this apparently progressive localization of theatrical activity, Norman E. Cameron, the man who is to be credited with having pioneered the rise of modern Guyanese drama, found cause to complain that no theatre with a positive Guyanese identity existed. He started writing plays in order to create such a theatre. But how valid was Cameron's claim at a time when popular performances were entertaining local audiences in Jamaica, Trinidad and Guyana ? A brief look at the history of Guyanese theatre may answer that question. It may also show where the story of this book of plays by Paloma Mohamed, which goes back to the source and uses the folk tale and folklore to impart lessons through drama, really begins.

It is instructive to survey the rise of theatre in the Caribbean region as a whole since the development of Guyanese theatre fits directly within that and all the English speaking Caribbean territories were subject to the same forces of social history that affected what took place on stage.

Dramatic plays were first performed in the West Indies in theatres in Jamaica in 1682. This was less than 30 years after British rule started in the island in 1655. There are no reliable records of theatre in the region during the Spanish occupation, quite likely because of the smallness of the Spanish population and because they took little interest in their West Indian colonies as important social environments. On the other hand, public theatre had just returned to England when the King regained control of the country after Puritan rule. The Puritans under Oliver Cromwell had imposed a ban on theatrical performances, but when his Commonwealth was defeated, local theatres opened in the colonies and touring theatre companies visited them to perform.

Jamaica soon became the capital of theatrical activity in the entire region and this was even officially recognized. An official post of Master (or Mistress) of the Revels was created and held by the person responsible to the Governor for all official entertainments and for overseeing the theatre. The island was host to several visiting professional companies from England and North America, especially during the War of Independence and the years of prohibition. The companies also visited other territories such as Antigua, Barbados, St. Lucia, Trinidad and Guyana, and the pattern was the same in all of them. Local companies and performers soon emerged and many new theatres were built. A very popular name for these houses was 'Theatre Royal', after the very famous Theatre Royal in Drury Lane, London, and the tradition that theatre and performing companies often existed under Royal patronage. These houses, however, did not survive, not only because the visiting companies had stopped coming by the end of the nineteenth century, but because the buildings seemed very susceptible to fires which repeatedly wiped them out.

The widespread imitation of English theatre names and tradition was significant for other reasons as well. The same tradition determined the content of the drama. The performers, whether visiting or local, were all British (or American) and their audience was the foreign ex-patriate population in the territories along with the local whites and coloureds. The plays were all European, and it took some time before new plays and dramatic pieces emerged written by local residents or reflecting any local environment. Moreover, performances were racially segregated, for whites only, with separate shows put on sometimes for 'persons of colour'.

Although the theatre buildings hardly survived into the twentieth century, the social attitudes and cultural / colour biases continued. The amateur theatre that gradually replaced the visiting professional companies was still dominated by the colonial colour and class traditions even though racial segregation dissipated. The plays were slowly absorbing local flavour and influences by the time vaudeville and popular shows in cinema houses had peaked.

It was even Longer before native Caribbean playwrights were using indigenous material and exploring myth and folklore the way Miss Mohamed does in this collection. Like most other cultural movements and traditions, however, it emerged gradually over a period of time, and although early twentieth century dramatists such as C.L.R.James, Una Marson, Archie Lindo and Ernest Cupidon did it, it was close to 1970 before major playwrights like Errol Hill, Derek Walcott, Dennis Scott followed by Trevor Rhone, Earl Lovelace, Rawle Gibbons and others found themselves exploring new forms informed by the oral traditions.

An interest in Caribbean folklore may, nevertheless, be seen among dramatists of previous centuries. Even during the years of elitism, foreign drama and segregation, local lore and legend attracted playwrights wherever they could use it within their own traditions and to fit the taste of their own audiences. Coleman's *The West Indian* (1771) exploited the exoticism, the awe and romance, and the mythical reputation of great wealth with which the people of London regarded sugar planters from the West Indies in the eighteenth century. Where real Caribbean folklore is concerned, plays were inspired by legends such as *Three Fingered Jack*, the story of *Orinooko and Imolinda* (the Royal Slaves of Guiana) and *Inkle and Yarico*, which originated in Barbados. Inkle and Yarico, originally a tale of injustice and tragedy, turned into folklore and myth, then into romance. It inspired dozens of versions in different languages across Europe between the seventeenth and nineteenth centuries. It is likely to be the most widely used of all West Indian tales in drama and poetry.

On occasions, European playwrights were distracted by such local subjects during these centuries, but it was not the norm. Even when this happened the dominant motif and form were those of the prevailing European dramatic types of the day. The common tradition that Norman Cameron confronted in Guyana in the 1930s was the tail-end of the long history of foreign oriented theatre in the colonies. Guyana, just like the rest of the English speaking Caribbean, experienced the visiting companies and the Theatres Royal. The fare was slightly more varied, however, because there is evidence of the theatre of two other linguistic groups, the Dutch and the Portuguese, to be found there. The Portuguese heritage is more important because of the strong tradition of musical performances and the many plays that they produced in the nineteenth century.

These had waned, however, by the time Cameron returned from his studies at Cambridge in England. Yet the plays were still mainly foreign; even those written by natives of British Guiana were imitative. The drama around the Caribbean had already been including local people and subjects, but primarily for comic effect. They were the butt of humour because of their quaint, if not backward, Creole speech, manners and folklore, and their low social stature. Playwrights could find nothing heroic about them and exploited their cameo presence in plays because their very appearance and rustic speech evoked laughter from an audience not yet at ease with local black persons on stage and because of a black population still suffering from self contempt.

At the same time the effects of Marcus Garvey's activities on behalf of the upliftment of black people were being felt across the Caribbean. There were organized groups and activities in Georgetown, which Garvey visited, devoted to a re-awakening of coloured people in the country. Similar movements were shaking the rest of the Caribbean, the working class was becoming organized, trade unionism was being born and the move to self-government was not far away. In this climate Cameron wrote his *Evolution of the Negro* and began to write plays in 1931 because he saw the need for drama that exhibited black people in a favourable and heroic light.

It was a period of nationalism and ethnic enlightenment in the colony of British Guiana. Another major group in the Guianese working class was the population of East Indian immigrants and their descendants. They represented another emerging force at the turn of the century, making the transition from the ranks of labourers to the educated middle class. Led by such men as Peter Ruhoman and Joseph Ruhoman, they were taking their place as intellectuals and professionals in the emerging society. By the 1940s there was a strong cultural group, the British Guiana Dramatic Society, promoting East Indian interests in Georgetown. While their performances were dominated by works from India, mainly those of Rabindranauth Tagore, they produced Basil Balgobin, their one playwright of note.

These activities in the theatre paved the way for local plays and playwrights who began to emerge later. The next major impetus was the founding of the Theatre Guild of Guyana, an amateur institution that was to have the greatest impact on the development of drama in Guyana, producing drama, playwrights, actors and directors, who have served Guyana and the rest of the Caribbean very well since then. The decade of the sixties presided over the emergence of most of Guyana's major established playwrights. As a direct result of the work of the theatre Guild, Frank Pilgrim and Sheik Sadeik developed. Around the same time Slade Hopkinson gained prominence, having worked with Derek Walcott's Trinidad theatre Workshop, and by the early seventies Michael Gilkes joined the ranks of the leading Guyanese dramatists. By the seventies, too, Michael Abbensettes became another major Guyanese playwright through a rising career in London where he had taken up residence.

The second line of playwrights in the Guyanese establishment is made up of a mixture of a newer generation of dramatists who are a part of the current wave of the country's contemporary theatre and two from the high days of the Theatre Guild. Francis Quamina Farrier became one of the country's most prolific playwrights to rise from that institution, while Bertram Charles worked largely on his own, rising in the 1970s. Then the most recent wave between 1980 and 2000 saw the rise of Ian Valz among the later contemporaries. The most influential dramatist in this generation, however, is Harold Bascom, who played a major part in the rise of popular theatre in this most recent period.

It is to this group that Paloma Mohamed belongs. She became involved in this 'take off' in local theatre while still a teenager, working among the several popular playwrights who came out of the last prolific period. A fairly precocious courage seemed to fuel talent and artistic ambition as she rose quickly to prominence as singer, poet, actress, then playwright and producer. She never lagged behind her elder colleagues, winning major awards in most of those capacities. As songwriter and singer, Miss Mohamed was once national champion, winning the right to represent Guyana at the Caribbean Regional Song Festival. She later won national awards as actress, followed by others for plays she wrote and directed. In drama, she claimed a place not only in the popular upheaval, but also among the most accomplished. Her tragic *Mamie* was selected to be Guyana's dramatic entry at Carifesta in Trinidad.

Having helped to popularise Guyanese theatre and benefited from the rise of the popular commercial plays, Bascom then advanced from the commercial to more serious stagecraft and twice won the prestigious Guyana Prize. So did Mohamed after him. Her interest in sophisticated stagecraft was evident very early in her career when she produced *Reggae Marley*, an attempt at the biography of Bob Marley. After that try to turn history into legend into theatre, her interest in folk material deepened even during her extended run of popular commercial plays. Arising from this interest, three important factors came together to produce this collection of drama. Mohamed's fascination for the didactic power of this art form, her developing study of the same quality in Caribbean folklore, and the fact that these could be combined to exploit mythology, the folk tale, and the folk characters as theatre and as education.

The use of these as dramatic elements cannot be taken for granted since it was very late in the history of Caribbean theatre that the oral traditions were recognized as theatre. Most historical or critical accounts do not accord them that stature, relegating them to such descriptions as 'meta-theatre' or 'pre-theatre', as merely 'theatrical' and the indigenous raw material from which Caribbean drama may be developed. A distinction is made between them and the 'art theatre', which is the formal or literary drama brought in from the European tradition; i.e. written plays as we have come to know them. Yet, the oral traditions have been the form of theatre practiced by the African population for as long as the 'art theatre' was practiced by the white colonists.

What is more, during the period of slavery and in the post-Emancipation era, they were regarded with suspicion by the colonial authorities. Performance traditions involving the playing of drums and dancing were often controlled by prohibitive legislation. However, since the beginning of the history of European drama in 1682, this theatre of the folk was performed as a parallel force. Then, with the arrival of Indian immigrants, the folk forms were diversified with the introduction of other traditions such as the *tadja*, which also suffered from curtailing laws, the *Ramleela* Tales and a tradition of *bhoj puri* songs in both Guyana and Trinidad. Gradually, these, as well as the popular cinema-house performances, began to influence the written drama, starting early in Jamaica and continuing across the Caribbean with the productions of Cupidon and Lindo, James and Marson, developing through Hill, Walcott, Scott and Rhone. In some cases, the playwrights experiment with forms borrowed from the folk traditions. The best known Guyanese play for this kind of debt to indigenous myth is Michael Gilkes' *Couvade*, which takes both name and shape from an Amerindian psychological state. Bascom's second Guyana Prize winner, *Makantali* (1996), inspired by a folk song, explores the legendary interiors of the porkknocker. Within the advance of these preoccupations, Guyana's drama is further fortified by Mohamed's exploitation of some of the qualities of myth and folklore characters as they function within their original communities.

It is therefore worthy of note whenever there is any important formal achievement in this area because it completes a cycle in the Caribbean theatrical act, while marking a frontier in the evolution of the stage. The employment of myth as form is a strength of *Duenne*, one of Miss Mohamed's plays, which is not included in this collection. *Duenne* is among Mohamed's best work and draws on a Trinidadian myth of African derivation. The *douen* is a Kalabari word which means 'the dead', an immaterial or spiritual form capable of dramatic imitation. In Trinidad it is the spirit of a child who dies before being named or christened and therefore not yet accepted in the world as a human being. It is potentially a harmful spirit, like the *abiku* of the Yoruba. The douen's feet are turned backwards, therefore one can be lost away if one follows what appears to be the footsteps of a child in the forest. Mohamed uses this 'child' figure in the play to take a dispassionate glance at the issue of abortion. This drama was declared Best Play, winning the Guyana Prize for Literature in 1998, while *Father of the Man*, another play by Mohamed, not included here, won the same award in 2000.

The plays in this collection dwell a bit more on the qualities of the fable. *Massacuraman*, more than the others, engages mythology in its use of the massacuraman, a feared demon figure who inhabits the Guyanese rivers and creeks. Despite his dreaded reputation, he is, in fact, a protector of the forest environment similar to the role played by Papa Bois of the Eastern Caribbean and Trinidad. Ironies, therefore, abound in the play. The villagers live in fear of the supernatural monster, but his anger is basically provoked by their own monstrous acts and abuses. This is sustained in the plot when the massacuraman is blamed for the villainy of one of the residents, then the damage done is atoned for by her self-sacrificing repentance.

Mohamed puts these one-act dramas forward as fables, in that they are teaching points from which the audience is expected to draw lessons. One may find in them the use of folk tale motifs, the 'culture trait' and, in particular, the 'culture hero'. A folk tale has several motifs, that is, small items that are included or that recur in the stories. A motif is regarded as the smallest unit into which the tale may be divided. A 'culture trait' is a particular phenomenon in the cosmology such as the fact that spiders live in the ceiling or that they are always spinning webs or that the turtle's back has marks all over it as if it is cracked up, or that there is a 'man in the moon'. A 'culture hero' is a folk hero or folk character who may cause change or causes things to happen. In many tales the culture hero is responsible for a particular culture trait coming into being. There is, however, a very important factor in the nature of a culture hero. While he might at times be mighty and triumphant because of his cunning, skill or intelligence, he is often a living representation of the characteristics of ordinary people who, because they are human, have vices and weaknesses. Despite the heroic qualities that the audience will expect him to have, he is often created to represent human behaviour. A folk hero can, therefore, meet a bad end in a story because of his greed. The lesson in the tale might be that success comes to those who have the capacity to be generous and selfless, so those who lack these qualities will fail.

Here are a few brief examples. Anansi is probably the most popular culture hero in the Caribbean. Most people regard him as a champion of the folk. While he lacks physical strength and political power, he has other qualities, which allow him to take on and beat strong and powerful adversaries like Tiger, tyrannical kings and even Brother Death, himself. Anansi has, above all, an excellent brain, which is his chief weapon. He is quick-thinking, creative and cunning. He is also magical because, while represented in the stories as a human being, he still retains the properties of a spider. On the other hand, like the worst of the human race, he is weakened by vices. He is greedy, selfish, lazy and cannibalistic, and there are stories in which these failings cause him to face defeat.

The folk tale explaining how the turtle's back came to be marked and cracked illustrates most of these features. Turtle is very much like Anansi, and is in fact, an Anansi substitute in several stories. The hard shell covering his back used to be smooth, with not a scratch on it. But because of his great avarice, he played a selfish trick on the birds, who were his friends, in order to get all their food for himself. In anger, they left him stranded in the sky. In order to get back to home on earth he had to skate on his back down from the highest mountain and, by the time he got to the bottom, his back was all scratched, marked and cracked up.

Here, the 'culture hero' was responsible for the circumstances that produced a 'culture trait'. The turtle's betrayal of his friends caused them to punish him, resulting in his back being marked up. While in this tale, the human vices of the hero are exposed, in most others, and in those explored by Mohamed, the positive qualities are stressed in order to teach the audience. Derek Walcott does the same thing in his well-known play, *Ti Jean and His Brothers*. Ti Jean is a St.Lucian folk hero with the good qualities of Anansi. He uses his wit and cunning to defeat the Devil and because of this, "God put him in the moon to be the sun's right hand, and guide the light of the world". It is commonly said that there is a man in the moon (a culture trait), and this tale explains how he got there because of the feats of Ti Jean (a culture hero).

Mohamed's one-act play, *Anansi's Way*, also draws on the good characteristics of the Anansi tradition in order to demonstrate to the audience the importance of literature, which always contains answers to human difficulties, non-violent ways of resolving problems, and the undying relevance of the wisdom of old traditions in dealing with new contemporary dilemmas. The hero, Nancy, who lacks great physical strength, like the culture hero whose name he takes, shows courage against the big bad bully in the school and eventually uses brain power to find a non-violent way to defeat him.

These kind of folk tale characteristics may be found in some of the other plays as well, and *A Fair Maids Tale* is a useful example. This draws on Guyanese Amerindian folklore as well as the social structure of the Amerindian community, which is strictly patriarchal. Men prove themselves by their achievements, heroism or the performance of some great deed for the benefit of the community. In this way they emulate benevolent demi-gods or god-heroes like Amalivaca or Pia. This kind of leadership and the role of benefactor are the domain of men and nothing of this nature is expected of women. The play goes into the very deep traditional setting in the world of myth to tell a story within that pastoral setting. But it is used to work out a modern concern for the place and role of women. The audience is expected to feel a sense of injustice and to challenge the paternalistic imbalance in the male disregard for women.

In the play, the heroine, Green Fern, is conscious that the men misuse power and this impresses itself upon her in the way her brother misuses the rod given to him as a gift by Makonima. She is convinced the gift should be used for the general good of the community. At the same time, she is convinced that a woman can achieve great deeds for the people just as good as men, and ventures out to prove it. She sneaks away the rod and, with the aid of its power, hauls in a great catch of fish. But the very men she wishes to impress disapprove of her good intentions and betray her, stealing her glory in order to establish themselves as heroes. She is left in despair and there is the over-riding impression that the society accepts that this kind of heroism is not her place. The Great Spirit takes pity on her and turns her into a goddess. As a goddess she can do good for her people and it will be accepted.

Some of the folk tale motifs may be found. Because of the heroine's good qualities, she is made a goddess as a reward and also to save her from an unhappy or tragic end. This is a very common motif in Greek mythology. The story may be seen as an explanation of how Green Fern became a goddess, which puts it in the realm of myth as explanation of cosmology. It goes further. Green Fern has the qualities that can enable an individual to succeed, but she is restricted by the environment within which she lives. In this society, achievement and great deeds are exclusively male preserves and her two major failings are that she is not male and that she dares to overstep her boundaries. In this way the play tries to make a modern or contemporary point, but dramatizes it by going into a traditional society. Green Fern recalls the character of Icarus in the Greek myth. Given a pair of artificial wings by his father, he ignores the warning not to fly too high because of his spirit of enquiry and discovery. But he over-reaches the boundaries imposed on mortal man and the sun causes him to fall by melting the wax that held his wings together. Yet, although he paid a penalty for his transgression, his kind of curiosity is progressive and the gods took pity on him

This kind of dramatization is not unknown in other mythologies such as the Hindu and in some East Indian communities in Guyana. These communities have adopted the story of heroine-goddess Sita, wife of the Hindu God–king-hero Rama. She is a symbol of purity as demonstrated in the events of her elevation. When she is accused of infidelity, she calls on the earth to open and take her in as a protestation of her innocence. The Earth Goddess appears and confirms her innocence, but chastizes the people, saying Sita is too pure to live among her accusers and takes her away. The same may be said of Green Fern in *A Fair Maid's Tale*. Her female sensibilities, her sense of justice and her knowledge of the betrayal of the community by the men they canonize, set her ahead of her time and above the conservative traditions of her unenlightened society.

A number of these same motifs are combined in *Sukanti* set in a Guyanese East Indian community and attempting to utilize some of their beliefs and traditions. But drawing some of these common practices into the plot is not as important or nearly as interesting as the dramatization of the tension between tradition and progress. This tension has already been explained as a major strength in *Massacuraman* and *A Fair Maid's Tale*. In *Sukanti*, the hero is a young man who took little interest in learning the family traditions, but assumes the role of a Sachulee, a wise fool, an Indian variant of the Anansi trickster figure, in his attempts to continue the family's attempts to arrange an advantageous marriage for his younger sister. But he fails at this just as he fails at performing the necessary religious rites. However, he is in possession of requisite qualities which rescue him from disaster and failure. Though in need, he resists greed and refuses to compromise principles for the lure of money. He repents his attempts to marry off his sister and, instead, sets about her education and improvement while seeking more creative ways out of their problems.

Mohamed allows modern enlightenment to triumph over inhibiting tradition in a way it does not quite happen in *A Fair Maid's Tale*. In part, Delicia offers the solutions to the difficulties encountered by Kishna and his sister. Her racial mix is symbolic. Not only is she a lesson against race hate aimed at Guyanese Blacks and Indians, but, being a mixture of both, she represents a new being, a rainbow, a suggestion that progress in the modern world is to be found in racial cooperation rather than bigotry.

This is also explored as a tension between the world of myth, folklore and superstition and the real world in which practical attitudes and a quest for progress deny the traditions they, themselves have created. Where belief is concerned, however, truth remains a mystery as Mohamed dramatizes in *Chupacabra* (Goat Sucker). She explains that the play was inspired by real events.

Years ago the Latin American world was gripped by a phenomenon that to this day has not been satisfactorily explained. There were popular allegations in Puerto Rico and Mexico of blood sucking kangaroos or space aliens that were stalking farms in these countries and killing countless livestock and poultry. In the 1920s there were also rumours of baby stealing and baby consumption taking place in the Dominican Republic. Of course, long before this, there were stories of vampire bats which killed cattle and people in Mexico.

Mohamed relates this to various Caribbean vampire types such as Ol Higue, Soucuyant and Firerass, bloodsuckers who drain their victims of blood, substance, and life. From these mythical creatures, she moves to the 'real life' Latin American reports and actual epidemics such as HIV/AIDS, which leave victims in similar states as those hit by demonic vampires.

This experimentation with indigenous material on the Guyanese stage represents the most recent phase in the evolution of the drama. It is not typical of contemporary Guyanese theatre since that is dominated by the popular plays, yet it demonstrates one of the directions in which theatre in the Caribbean has developed. The theatre has gone back to its indigenous roots after a long history of colonialism and segregation. The rise of the popular theatre in the region and the radical popularisation of theatre in Guyana, which came much later, widened the path to the several possibilities available to dramatists and, among the contemporaries, Paloma Mohamed takes advantage of those possibilities.

The publication of this collection of plays is a notable achievement for another reason. It is among the relatively few published collections of recent Caribbean drama, joining the *Calypso Trilogy* (2000) by Rawle Gibbons of Trinidad. They stand alone as collections rooted in the oral tradition and popular culture, but Mohamed's publication is unique because it was designed for a school audience. Its deliberate didactic intentions might tend to make it a more difficult task to accomplish, but the significant element is its return to the fable and the folk tale tradition. A major function of this tradition is education. It has always been used to teach succeeding generations in the oral tradition long before written literature, before the arrival of European drama in the Caribbean and throughout the centuries when the working people of the region were practicing it but the critical accounts were not recognizing it as theatre. This recognition is now taking shape with each production of a play inspired by the oral tradition, like those in this collection.

Al Creighton
University of the West Indies

Cave Hill, Barbados
Summer, 2003.

Al Creighton is a well known arts critic and cultural commentator. His reviews have been published in the Stabroek News (Guyana) and London Times among others. Creighton is a published poet and essayist as well as a prize-winning dramatic director. He has been Deputy Vice Chancellor, Dean of the Faculty of Arts and Dean of the Department of Amerindian Studies at the University of Guyana. Creighton has been chairman of the panel of judges for the Guyana Prize for Literature and also judge of the Commonwealth Writers Prize. He is currently the head of the National School of Drama in Guyana.

LIST OF ILLUSTRATIONS

Bloodsuckers
Massacuraman
Sukanti –
Anansi
Fair Maid and Makonaima

NOTES ON SET DESIGN AND STAGING OF THESE PLAYS

The sets and settings described for most plays in this book may seem complex at first glance. They are not meant to be laboriously followed. The details and descriptions are meant more as a kind of geographic and psychic locator since the material, characters and the places where the work is set may be difficult to visualize otherwise. This will definitely be true of non-Caribbean people but it is also likely to be true for many people who live in the region but who have no experience of the places, issues and characters in these plays. The sets and settings are the ideal.

Too much emphasis is not to be placed upon their realistic construction however. Certainly, if there are resources and a director and students make such a choice it could be wonderful. For school productions, I would like to stress the use of minimal sets with symbolic reference points and the creative use of bodies as another way of representing sets, once the requirements are understood from my descriptions.

For instance, *Chupacabra* only requires one large tree. *A Fair Maid's Tale* however, speaks of functional rivers, mountains and a jungle. How is the novice director to represent these seemingly impossible requirements on stage? The functional river can be represented by students undulating stretches of cloth at points when the river is needed. The mountains need be nothing more than ladders or boxes placed behind *papier mache* facades or even plants. The forest can be a group of students dressed as trees or otherwise moving a drawing of a forest scene or backdrop. When The Massacuraman was performed in Guyana and Jamaica , the Essequibo river a very cheap, small inflatable swimming pool was used behind a painted cardboard ramp.

In other words, there are creative, in-expensive and workable ways of creating the sets for *all* of the plays in this book. The interpretation and creation of working sets with limited resources is an opportunity to involve students with different talents than those of performing or even art into the creative theatrical process. Don't be afraid to be creative!

Chupacabra
A Play in One Act
Paloma Mohamed

Chupacabra – Modern blood sucking being or beast that is said to have attacked mostly animals during the mid 1990's in Puerto Rico, Mexico and other Latin American countries.

Characters:
Vetala - Indian (Male)
Obayifo - African (Male or female)
Chedipe- Indian woman riding a Tiger
Cuitatato - The Mexican Princess
Logaroo - Male (Haiti & Grenada)
Chaing Shih - Chinese (Male)
Jaracaca- Brazil (Male)
Asema - Cuban (Female)
Ol Higue - Guyanese (Female)
Socuyant - Trinidad (Female)
Jada - Teenage girl
Jarrel - Teenage boy
Chucapabra – Latin (Male)

Set: A large Silk Cotton tree at the point where four cross-roads meet. Several large copper pots, cauldrons, clay jars and dark bottles strew the landscape like large rocks and stones.

Setting: Dead of night.

Action : Between 10pm and Midnight. The whole play takes places as a continuous sequence of events. Once it begins there are no indications of scene endings or beginnings. Indications of different scenes are simply for formatting purposes.

Scene 1

Lights up on the set. Dead silence then a loud thud as Socuyant falls from the sky barely missing the tree.

Socuyant: Aiiiiiiiiiiiiiiiiiiiiiiieeeeeee! *(Gets up hurriedly and brushes herself off.)* Not me you see! Not me eh!

Obayifo: *Rising out of a large jar. Laughs.)* Dey ketch you too?!

Socuyant: *Jumps)* Ayeeeeeee!

Obayifo: *Laughs)* If you had a skin you woulda jump right out of it !

Socuyant: *Looks around)* Where my skin?! Where it? Where it?!

Oba: Cool it Socuyant Girl! You will find it!

Socu: But suppose somebody find it! Suppose they pepper it! Suppose....

Oba: Just calm down and think where you left it...

Socu: I left it here! Right here! Obayifo! Woman! You tief my skin?!!

Oba: *Gives a long stewps.)* Look me! *(Extends her arms)* This lovely black skin could ever be yours?!

Socu: You see it Oba? You see it?!

Oba: No but we bound to find it. Only you an me here. *(They begin to look.)*

Socu: But you travel far! What you doing in these parts?!

Oba: Girl! I is you great-great-great grandmother! I could go wherever I want!

Socu: Yes! But what you doing *here*?!

Oba: *Sighs loudly.)* If I tell you...if I tell you....

Enter Logaroo stumbling blindly and spitting violently.

Logaroo: Ah! Ohhhhhhhhh! Ohhhhhhhhhhhhh! Helllllllll!

Oba and Socu: Logaroo?! What you doing here?!!!

Logaroo: *Spits more furiously and collapses on the floor.)*

Socu: Logaroo! This is not you territory! How you find yourself here?

Logaroo: Ah...Ah... problems in Haiti and Grenada....

Oba and Socu : *Exchange glances.)*

Oba: *What* kinda problems you talking about?

Logaroo: *Spits again.)* Hell! The bitches almost poison meh!

Jaracara swings down from the Silk Cotton tree.

Jaracara: *Laughs)* For you this is good! Feast on the milk of the breast we tell you. For generations we tell you. But no! These people they are stubborn! The poison they must take! They are stubborn!

Logaroo: Oh shut up! *(Spits again)* You come here from Brazil with you snobbery again! Last time we meet up I tell you! No self respecting.....!

A Church bell chimes ten times.

Socu and Oba: Ahhhhhhhhhhhhh! *(Covering their ears. They begin to count compulsively .)* One-two-three-four-five-six-seven-eight-nine-ten-one-two....

Jara: *Claps his hands sharply.)* Oh! Snap out of it you two!

Socu and Oba: Almost out of breath stop counting.)

Oba: Ah! Ah!

Socu: Jara, Thanks...

Jara: Shhhh! *(Sniffing the air)* She comes. The Princess. Ahhh!

Oba: Here? You mean Cuitatato coming here?!

Jara: Yes.

Oba: But she must be mad!

Logaroo: Why she had to be mad? This is the crossroads. Is no mans land! It ent belong to nobody!

Oba: *Gives him a powerful look.)*

Logaroo: Your looks can't kill me! I have the same powers as you Oba!

Socu: Oh Gord! We have guest... alyuh behave nah!

Logaroo: Must be *you* who have guests. Right now I can't entertain nobody!

Enter Ciitatato. She stands at the center of the cross roads attempts to cross to the right but is unable to go further.

Ciuta: I am here.

Jara: Welcome Princess! Welcome!

Oba: Well! What ill wind blow you here?

Cuita: There is a conference they say.

Logaroo: Yuh radar mix up Cuita! No conference!

Cuita: What do you all do here, then?

Socu: Well I for one just ... *land* here by accident!

Jara: Out of the sky he fell. Boops! Just like this! On the way home!

Logaroo: *Laughs.)*

Oba: Well *you* don't laugh! Not after dey almost poison and kill *you*!

Jara: Disoriented. This one. Disoriented. From the poison, no?

Logaroo: Well since you know about everybody, tell us about you?

Jara: I....I...ah....

Cuita: There was a meeting you said!

Jara: *Slyly)* Ah...well...Si...yes.... between you and me !

Cuita: *Growls)* Jara! I have told you times more than a million si? I have not time for the men now! None! *(Turns to go.)*

Jara: But Princess....

Oba: Oh! Let the woman go. This is not her territory anyway!

Cuita: *Turns around) What* did you say?

Oba: I said you don't belong here!

Cuita: I am the Princess! I have more rights here than you!

Oba: Never! All you all come from me! Logaroo, Socuyant, Ol Higue .....

Enter Ol Higue.

Ol Higue: Somebody call me?

Cuita: *Groans)* Bloody commoner!

Socu: Jeez! Anywhere dey have a set a woman it must have trouble! Not me you hear! Not me! *(Begins to search again)* The minute you see I find my skin, I outa here!

Ol Higue: Somebody call me?

Oba: I call yuh *name* child. I didn't mean for you to come!

Ol Higue: But as I here. You all sharing food or what?

Logaroo: Hoooooooooooo! How I can't take dese beggars and them!

Jaca: Why you pretend this way? You are hungry as well!

Logaroo: Yes! Well...but have some manners nah? You can't ask for food as soon as you reach a place!

Oba: She come far-far. Guyana. Come my great-granddaughter. Come I never set eyes on you from you born. Come let this old woman see you....

Cuita: Careful with she ! That old woman does suck anything she can catch!

Oba: You come here looking for trouble or what?

Cuita: No. But you are known. The Higue must be warned.

Oba: Advancing on her.)

Cuita: Come witch! We Spanish never back down from a fight! *(Tries to cross the line of the cross roads but cannot.)*

Oba: *Laughs wickedly.)* Pity yuh foot tie!

Cuita: Enough Oba! I said it is enough!

Logaroo: Ow. Stop nah. I am a sick man....

Oba: Princess in a prison! That's what you are!

Cuita: *Lets out a loud shriek and hurls some corn from inside her pockets at Oba.)*

Oba: *Screams loudly. Bend and begins to pick up the corn counting as she goes along.)*

Soucu, Logaroo and Ol Higue compulsively join her.)

Jara: Princess. Have a heart. Look what you have done to them. The innocent and the guilty all are condemned to the counting.

Cuita: That Oba she is too full of herself! She asked for it, the corn!

Jara: *Claps his hands three times.)*

All those counting snap out of it with large sighs and moans.)

Cuita: *Turning away)* Fool. I was loving that!

Enter Chaing Shih. He bows and takes a seat with his legs and arms crossed.

All the others watch him in silence as he arranges himself.

Chaing : I am a little late. Sorry.

All the others continue to watch him in incredulous silence.

Chaing: Well...where is everyone else?

Socu: Well I can't believe my eyes! A Chinee vampire ?!

Oba: I guess we really shouldn't ask. Somebody invite you to a meeting?

All turn to look at Jara.

Jara: But it was not me! Most definitely ! Not me!

Cuita: So *Chaing Shih*, is that the right pronunciation? *Who* told you about this meeting?

Chaing: The Indians.

Oba, Socu, Ol Higue, Jara and Cuita: *The Indians?!!*

Enter Chedipe leading her Tiger. She is carrying an ornate box which she sets down. From it Vetala emerges.

Chedipe : *Gives namaste and sits upon her Tiger.*)

Socu: Auntie!

Oba: Auntie?!!

Socu: Ah...I must confess. I am a Dougla!

Ol Higue: Me too!

Oba: *Hisses and spins away.*)

Vetala: Looks around.) Everybody here?

Chaing: I Chaing, am here. I have travelled far from China.

Cuita: I am Cuitala. Princess! I bring greetings from Mexico and Latin America!

Oba: *Whispering to Logaroo.*) Show off! Well I guess I better bring greetings from Africa!

Socu: I am Socuyant, Mistress of the night and resplendent fire, and wondrous might and....

All: Ok.ok.ok!

Socu: Queen of Trinidad and Tobago!

Logaroo: And I am Logrooo. The eastern Caribbean islands are mine!

Chedipe: Namsaste, brothers and sisters. I am Chedipe. From India.

Vetala: Northern India...

Chedipe: Sorry. Yes. Northern India.

Jara: I am Jara. Hailing from the beautiful Brasilia!

Ol Higue: I am Ol Higue, daughter of night and eternal flame. I come from Guyana.

There is a pause.)

Vetala: Is that everyone?

There is another pause. All turn to look at OBA.

Oba: You think *I* need an introduction?

Vetala: I am Vetala master of the mysteries of death. From India. I bring a message also from Count Dracula…he is most ill. He apologizes, much too weak to travel he says.

There is a pause. All turn to look at Oba once again.

Oba: Ok! I am Oba! Mother of the undead! Keeper of the mystery of life and death! High priestess of the fire and I , I hold Africa like a grain of sand in my hand!

All Clap. Except Cuitala.

Cuitala: Oh! Please!

Oba: *Pleased bows.*)

Chedipe: So we are in esteemed company.

Oba: *Bows again.*)

Chaing: Vetala, I am most concerned. We have not all met like this for three hundred years!

Oba: *Gives a signal with her hands.*)

Lights change to deep red.

Scene 2

Low staccato drums beating. All gathered chant:

All: Blood is life and life is Blood!

Jara: *Puts up his hand tentatively.*)

All Freeze.

Jara: Ah…might I abstain from reciting this creed?

All: *Ignoring him*)   Blood is life and life is blood!
                                  Blood is power and spirit!
                                  Blood is life and life is blood!
                                  Blood is power and spirit!

Jara: All this talk of blood! It...makes me sick!

All: *Continue to chant.)*

Jara: Truly! Do you not think it is time to change your diet?

Vetala: Blood is the secret to life, Jara! Not breast milk!

Cuita: Hurry! It is fast approaching the hour when the elements of heaven and earth will meet and you speak of milk?

Oba: *Laughs)* Midnight!

Jara: But why did you call us here? Some us have a long way to go....

Chaing: Yes! Before the sun returns we must return!

Vetala : I too have the same concerns. But do you think I would venture so far from home for the ride? The situation is serious!

Jara: What situation?!

Chedipe: We find our existence in danger....

Chaing: Our very existence threatened after all these millennia!

Socu: *Laughs)* You mean we joining the list of endangered species?!

Oba: So why you say we endangered?

Ol Higue: That easy! Nobody don't believe in we no more!

Chaing: *Sneering)* Just because they don't believe does not mean we don't exist!

Vetala: Yes. Yes. I am afraid it is not a question of belief. It is the precious blood, our supplies. I am afraid it has been infiltrated by what I believe is a small vampire-like creature not like our species.

Chedipe: It is so small that the eye cannot see, so strong that nothing can kill it, so selfish that it does not discriminate.

Logaroo: Wait, wait. What you all talking in parables. What is actually going on?!

Vetala: The blood of the people of the world is becoming increasingly ....shall we say....

Chaing: Contaminated?

Vetala: *Nods.)*

Oba: So that's it?! That's what's happening! I thought it was only in Africa!

Socu: Ah! Now I get the answer! That's what you doing here! Poaching!

Vetala: Sadly all over India the situation exists too.

Chedipe: *Nods)* Yes sister. I noticed it twenty years ago. The young men, when I visit their homes in the night, I no longer had to cast my sleeping spell upon them. They sleep as death itself...as death *(Shudders).*

All : *Shudder)* Ohhhhhhhhh!

Chedipe: Yes. But worse when I take the toes into my mouth and drink my fill. The next night I feel so weak...so weak...

Socuyant: It is the same with me! The blood is like it not good no more. Make me so weak, I can hardly fly....messing up my radar...missing key hole and *ting....*

Logaroo: I have to pick an' choose. And still less and less people to choose in dem small islands. They dying like files and I swear is not me killing them!

Ol Higue: Oh! So that's what it is! The blood contaminate! And I thought I was just getting old!

Oba: In Africa it is so bad. By the thousands they die. There are so few left and my powers can't guide me to the safe ones. But I thought it was only there....

Chaing: China. Same thing. Blood bad. Life short. Terrible thing!

Vetala: Dracula says the same in Euroupe and America! Ah! A terrible thing!

Jara: See! Same thing! Long time now, I tell you. My friends, forget this bloodsucking and drink the milk of the breast. Like me!

All: *Stare icily at him.*

Jara: Well...it was just a suggestion....

Cuita: Silly beings! There is no problems. Leave the adults. That has been my policy for centuries. We have free access to the children and babies!

Oba: *Grinning)* Yes! The newest, freshest lives of all!

Vetala: Those too carry the plague.

Cuita: *Draws a deep breath)* Babies?! And children too?!

Chedipe: Some children born of a mother with the killer in her blood. They too carry it...

Cuita: Some! Some you say?

Vetala: Yes. Not all. But some babies.

Cuita: Well then there is no problem!

Chaing: Yes...but only a small one....

Cuita: A problem?

Chaing: Can you tell the ones who carry it from the ones who don't dear Princess?

Oba: *Laughs)* We are all in the same boat Cuita! You no better off than we!

Cuita: Oh! What is to become of me then?!

Ol Higue: Of us. What is to become of us?

Jara: This is the end! I can see it!

All: Stare at him icily.)

Jara: Well... for you ! Not for me.... !

O Higue: Fool! You can't see? If everybody dying nobody will be left to make even breast milk for you?!!

Jara: Ah! Ahhhhhhhhhh! I did not think. This is True! It is true! Ah! What...what will we do?

Enter Asema.

Asema: Do about what?!

Jara: *Heloooo!* Long time no see *you*!

Cuita: *Hisses loudly.)*

Jara: No to be jealous my Princess. Just saying hello!

Asema: What is going on here? Why did you call me?

Oba: We are discussing a problem.

Asema: I have no problem.

All: What?!

Asema: *Preparing to leave)* No. Nada. Ningun.

Vetala: You mean the situation in Cuba is good? No plague?

Asema: Plague? What are you talking about?

Jara: It lives in the blood. Hides there long and poisons and kills *(Looks around at others)*...At least that's what they say!

Asema: A plague of the blood?! I have not heard of this.

Logaroo: Then we have a solution. Lets all relocate to Cuba and live happily ever after!

Cuita: If this thing is present in India, Africa, China, America, Europe, Latin America, here in the Caribbean, all over the world, they could not escape it! It is impossible! She lies!

Asema: I lie? To what end?!

Cuita: Witches have no reason to lie. It is natural as blood sucking to us.

Asema: Speak for yourself!

Cuita: I am no witch! I am The Princess!

Socu: Ladies! Witches! Bitches! We are trying to discuss our problem....

All: Yes!

Chaing: And the moon is waning fast!

All: *Shuddering)* Yes....

Ol Higue: And the sun will approach from the east...the direction in which I have to fly!

Chedipe: So lets not waste time!

Vetala: We can see that leaving our homes, flying from place to place will bring no end to our misery.

Oba: We find it everywhere we go...a trail of sickness and lingering death...which even we cannot countenance....

Logaroo: Look tonight! I almost get poison ! Is a damn problem in truth!

Chaing: Hmmmmmmmmm. Does this...this scourge have a name?

Ol Higue: Does it...have a name?

Chedipe: What is wrong? Are we afraid to name it?

Logaroo: If it so terrible we might ketch it from just saying the name....

Oba: Don't be stupid! It in the blood! Not in the air boy! Is only from mixing blood and blood it could live.

Asema: Well name it then!

Socu: Right! Name it then!

Oba: Ah....

Cuita: Yes! Since you so old and wise...

All: *In rising crescendo)* Name it! Name it! Name it Oba! Name it!

Oba: Alright! Alright! Alright! A......

The clock chimes eleven. All look up to the sky and shudder as the lights turn to purple.

Socu, Oba, Logaroo, Oh Higue and Asema all begin to count: One-two-three four-five-six-seven-eight-nine-ten-eleven-one-

Vetala and Chaing exchange glances.

Vetala: What is going on with them?!

Cuitala: They have this counting thing that they have to do.....

Chedipe: Well when are they going to stop?

Jara: Not till somebody stops them!

Vetala: How?

Jara: Usually some good licks with a Pointer broom does the trick! But I find a few short claps will suffice.

Chedipe: *Claps a few times in rapid succession.*)

The counting stops.

Scene 3

Socu, Oba, Logaroo, Oh Higue and Asema are all breathless.

Chaing: *To Oba*) Madame. If you will oblige us with the name...when you catch your breath?

Oba: Yes...yes...

A light approaches in the distance.

Chedipe: *Screams*) The Sun! It rises!

Socu: *Trembling*) What trouble is this? And I ent find my skin ! (*Hides herself in a big jar.*)

As the light comes closer all the others shriek and run for cover. Secreting themselves in any way they can among the debris and rocks. The light comes closer and closer and footsteps are heard.

Enter Jarrel and Jada. Jarrel is holding a torchlight in this left hand. His right arm is around Jada's shoulders.

Jada: *Shudders.*)

Jarrel: *Pulling her closer*) You cold?

Jada: All of a sudden, I just feel a chill....

Jarrel: Me too. Some cold breeze passing. But we don't have far to go to reach the main road.

Jada: I am enjoying the time alone with you. The walk is not tiring. Is just this place of the four roads. You know what they say?

Jarrel: You listen to your grandmother and she old wives tales too much! Nothing else don't happen here that don't happen anywhere else.

Jada: *Shivers again*) Still. I don't like it out here. And this old jumbie tree....

Jarrel: *Laughs*) Oh! Come on! You know you don't have nothing to fear. Your Jarrel is here!

They stop to kiss and Jarrel lowers the torchlight.

Chiang: *Springs up*) Ah! At last dinner!

Chedipe: Ohhh! Look at those lovely *toes*! I saw them first remember!

Logaroo: Fool! You **see** a torchlight and thought it was the sun! Just for that you don't deserve none!

Oba: *Stepping forward*) Elders first!

Ol Higue: We can share....surely we can share...

They all begin to converge on the unsuspecting couple licking their tongues and hissing as they move forward. They reach within striking distance .

Jara: *Swinging down from the tree*) But suppose these two have the killer blood?

All freeze.

Jara: Just a question....

Jarrel and Jara: *Begin to walk again.*

Chedipe: *Growls*) He is a young and virile male! Look at him!

Socu: And the girl. Fresh and rosy like a doux-doux mango!

All except Jara: They don't look sick!

They all advance again.

Jara: But you can't see inside the blood!

All freeze.

Vetala: He is right.

Ol Higue: But they look sooooooo healthy!

Logaroo: Just like the one who nearly poison me tonight! *(Spits in memory.)* Was looking even rosier than these two! *(Turns away.)*

Chaing: But I have travelled far (*Advancing.*) I need sustenance before the sun arrives and banishes me again !

Cuita: It is not my business what you do brother Chiang. But it seems a terrible risk!

Jara: Yes. Like a game of blind mans bluff! You don't know who carries the thing that kills by just looking!

Chaing: *Still advancing .)* But just a drop a tiny drop....pleaseeeeeeee!

Vetala: *Turning away.)* At your own risk!

Jada and Jarrel walk off and Chaing sinks to the floor in disgust.) Arghhhhhhhhhhhhh! I let them go! I let them go!

Asema: Better safe than sorry Chaing.

Vetala: Even I almost lost control and forgot the danger.

Oba: Me too!

Logaroo: We must thank our brother Jara yet again!

Jara: *Bows.)*

Asema: This problem. It remains. What are we to do?

Ol Higue: The key is people...normal people...not like us....

Logaroo: How you mean *people*? They dying! The thing killing them! Like you don't get it?!!

Ol Higue: I do. That's why we have to save them!

Logaroo: *Laughing)* We?! Ol Higue and Logaroo, and Socuyant and all these blood sucking beings? *We? Save* people?!! Like you forget who we is or what?!

Asema: Stop being ignorant! Sister is right, If we allow the people to die...then we have to face death too....

All: Shudder.)

Logaroo: Oh...ok. (*To Ol Higue*) Well why you jus' din say that?!

Chaing: Hmmmmmmmmmm. Stop the thing in the blood....that's what we have to do!

Cuita: We have no power inside the blood! We can't do nothing!

Asema: How does it get into the blood in the first place?!

Oba: They say it pass from one person to another, through a cut or a puncture or a sore or a wound or a needle....

All: Ohhhhhhhhhhhh! Through a break in the skin!

Socu: You mean the puncture hole ?

Vetala: *Nods.*)

Asema: So our teeth, they act like the needles then?!

Oba: Yes. So then one blood mix with the other blood and then it happen.

Asema: What one have the other get.

Logaroo: Just like that?

Chaing: Evidently!

Vetala: Hmmmmmmmmmm.

Jara: So the answer is to keep that killer blood from passing on and on and on then?

Cuita: Brilliant! I think he has the answer!

All : Yes! Keep the killer blood from passing from one person to the other!

Chaing: It is not blood itself that is killing.

All stare at him.)

Chaing: It is a killer *living* in the blood!

All: Ah! Yes! Blood is life and life is blood! It is a killer living in the blood!

Logaroo: Down with the killer living in the blood!

All: Down with the killer living in the blood!

Logaroo: Down with it ! Down with it!

All: Down with it ! Down with it!

Vetala: *Begins to twitch uncontrollably. Brings himself under control and signals for quiet.*) Do we agree that this thing in the blood is our common enemy?

All: Yes! Down with it!

Asema: Then we must think of how to stop it!

All: Yes! We must stop it!

Jara: But how?

All: Huh?

There is an uncomfortable pause.

Vetala: *Twitching again. Brings himself under control.*) There are those of you who are still of the human plane and those of us who are not....

Oba: We of the flesh we live among people by day .....

Chaing: And we of the spirit we roam the nether world.....

Cuita: We can speak through dreams....

Socu: And we can have real conversations.....

Asema: We must combine our talents!

All: Yes!

Socu: Leave no stone unturned!

All: None!

Chaing: Cuita, Chedipe, Vetala, Jara and I, we will visit people in dreams! Tell them that a killer is lurking to enter their blood. We will warn them to be careful who they share blood with and to keep their bodies as sanctuaries!

Oba: And Oh' Higue, Socuyant, Logaroo, Asema and me. We will talk to people young and old, tell them about this thing that could kill them painful and slow. Worse than when Ol Higue attack you!

Chedipe: We will frighten away young lovers who lust without thinking!

Vetala: Yes! We will speak in their ears, blow cold winds upon them, intrude on their thoughts until they learn to stop themselves.

Ol Higue: We will tell them horrible stories of the millions who have died, so young, so alone, prematurely and in their best blooming years!

Cuita: All over the world we will tell the mothers , their babies could perish too! (Turning away) Like mine did so long ago (*Sobs.*)

Socu: We will tell grandmothers and grandfathers, that is not like tax! They not exempt!

All: Far and wide! Night and day! In spirit and in flesh! We going to tell them! There is a killer
waiting to get into your blood! A killer trying to invade your blood! A killer trying to snuff out your life ! A killer name ......name (*All look at Oba*) Oba! What the damn thing name?!

Vetala: *Begins to twitch again. This time he is unable to bring himself under control and rises and begins to move about as if he is being yanked by an invisible rope).* No! No! I am not going!

All: *Exchange glances.*

Socu: Like somebody trying to contact "V"!

Chedipe: *Nods.)* Excuse *me.(Opens the box and pushes Vetala in and sits on the lid. The box moves around violently.)*

Logaroo: Why you obstructing the man business then? If they calling him, let him go!

Ol Higue: You don't see he don't want to go?!

Oba: If that is his work. He have to do it!

Chedipe: All who doing this kind of work have to be careful these days. Those who they send them to kill might kill them instead!

All: True! True!

The box settles down.

Chedipe: *Opens it and lets Vetala out.)*

Vetala: Emerges disheveled and exhausted.

Socu: Like it was a real fight boy!

Vetala: *Nods. Panting.)* Can't go where people send me just like that nowadays! Dangerous! Very Dangerous!

Chaing: Yes. I can see the problem...the blood again!

Asema: *Introspectively.)* Then I too must think about the summons I answer.

Scene 4
There is a loud clap of thunder and followed by a bolt of lightening.

Cuita: *Looks up at the sky)* Huh!

Another Clap of thunder .

Oba: *Looks up into the sky and laughs crazily)* You?! You again?!

A louder clap of thunder.)

Oba: You not tired ? Every time we meeting you sending rain and lightening? Thundering disapproval at the top of your voice?!

Socu: Oba! Take it easy eh! Don't provoke them. We standing under a tree. They could send lightening to strike it!

Oba: Send it! Send it! Do you worse! We want to live forever just like you! But in the flesh! In the flesh!

Chaing: And in the spirit...but in this world...not in yours!

All: Chanting: Life is sweet if life is long!
           We too young to be struck down!
           We too strong to be stuck down!

The rain comes pouring down. All start to shriek and spit at the sky.

Enter Jada and Jarrel running back from the direction from which they exited. They seek shelter under the tree.

The creatures withdraw to the shadows.)

Jada: God! This look like a big thunderstorm brewing Jarrel. You sure we shoulda turn back ?

Jarrel: Yes! This is a safe place. The tree will give us shelter. There was no shelter anywhere else for miles.

Jada: I still feel if we continued we woulda reach home before long.

Jarrel: *Putting his arm around her and pulling her close.)* I find you hurry to get home! Like you running away from me or something?

Jada: No! But it late and my Grandmother will be looking out and worrying after me!

Jarrel: You safe. You safe here with me! (*Kisses her and continues further.*)

Jada: Jarrel. We shouldn't be doing this...

Jarrel: I love you. I will love you till the end of eternity. You don't have *nothing* to fear with me....

Jada: I feel the same way about you too (*They continue to kiss and grope until they are lying on the ground.*)

Souc: Well! Same thing I say. It about to happen! So much for the talk about dreams and abstain!

Asema: He's right! We should do something....

Chaing: You mean to stop them? Sex a niceeeeeeeee thing!

Socu: Yes! But nowadays it could get yuh kill!

Chedipe: No sex?! This is worse than it sounds!

Ol Higue: You all only talking while them two young people going really far!

Oba: Grinning.)Allow me. (*Steps out into the shadows as an old woman with a stick. She comes to the place where the two are about to commit the act.*)

Jada and Jarrel are startled .)

Oba: Night!

Flash of lightening.)

Jada: Miss Benjamin?! Good night (*Fixes herself self consciously.*)

Jarrel: *Whispering)* You know that woman?

Jada: Yes. Miss Benjamin from up the street!

Jarrel: *To Oba.)* Ah..Goodnight...

Oba: This look like a good night to you?

Jarrel : Ah...no...I ...is a really bad night!

Oba: That why you trying to kill one another out here?

Jada: Kill? Miss Benjamin what you talking about?!

Oba: Ain't you all was going to do it right here in the mud tonight?!

Jarrel: What?!

Oba: Aint you was going to do it without protection?

Jarrel: What protection?

Oba: Unfurls her stick into an umbrella.) Protection ! To cover your …!

Jada: Ok! Ok!

Jarrel: Look Old lady....

Oba: No you look! You look! (*Flashes her stick at Jada.*)

Jada: *Turns pale. Cries weakly*) Help me...Jarrel...help me...it hurts so much...(*Coughs.*)

Jarrel: *Screams*) Oh! God! Jada! Jada! What happen to you?

Oba: *Laughs.*) Yuh didn't use protection!

Jarrel: What? We didn't do nothing!

Oba: But if I didn't turn up?

Jarrel: You...you old witch ! What did you do? What did you do to her?!

Oba: Not me! You! What you do to she?

Jarrel: I did not do that! I tell you! No!

Oba: Go on like this, no protection and three years from now, six months, ten years...you would kill she. Or she would kill you.

Jarrel: Me?! She woulda kill me like...*that*? (*Points to Jada.*)

Oba: Whatever you have you will give she. Whatever she have you will get. If you do it with no protection you courting death!

Jada: *Gasps for air as if she is drawing her last breath.*)

Jarrel: Jada! Jada. Please ...please don't die! Please don't....

Jada: *Coughs and gets up healthy as she was before.*) Jarrel. What happen to you? Why you crying?

Jarrel: Jada? (*Hugs her*) You ok! You not sick?!

Jada: Of course I ok! *You* ok? You suddenly acting weird?!

Jarrel: *Looking around*) Where that old woman ? Where she?

Oba has rejoined the others in the shadows.*)

Jada: Who knows. Them old people strong. She will walk through this rain and reach home and tell my Grandmother about me and you.
Jarrel: *Shudders*) I think we better get going too.

Jada: *Holding onto him.*) Why we don't stay until the rain finish ? Then we could finish what we just started?

Jarrel: No! I...I ...Jada. I think we should...I just don't think it's a good idea you know.

Jada: *Persistent*) But it was feeling good. We can't stop now....

Jarrel: Look! It too cold. My clothes too wet....

Jada: Well . Just take them off....

Jarrel: *Resists a little and then begins to give in.*)

The creatures in the background react in horror.

Chaing: It does not work !

Vetala: It has to work! We have to stop them!

Logaroo: It is a waste! If we stop them this time. They will do it some other time!

Asema: He is correct or course.

Ol Higue: But we can't just give up after one try!

Jara: True!

Chaing: Allow me.... (*Steps off from the group and stands very still.*)

Jada: *Holds her head and cries out.*) Ahhhhhh!

Jarrel: Jada? What's the matter?

Jada: Ahhhhhh! Oh my god! Ohhhhh! Poor Jarrel! Poor Jarrel! And poor Jada!

Jarrel: Jada? What's wrong...what are you seeing?

Jada: *Rising.*) The future Jarrel...the future. (*Walks out into the rain.*)

Jarrel: Where are you going?

Jada: Home.

Jarrel: *Follows her. Holds her by the shoulders and turns her around.*) You saw it too? The agony and dying?

Jada: Yes!

Jarrel: Sighs) It's ok. We can wait....

Jada: You mean it? You will wait with me and be with me only?

Jarrel: Yes. (*Puts his arm around her.*) I want us to live! (*They walk off.*)

The creatures emerge from the shadows hooting and shrieking in delight.

Logaroo: It worked!

Cuita: We solved the problem!

Jara: Really?

All stare at him in silence.

Jara: There is this small question of supplies in the meantime?

Chaing: Ah! Yes....supplies.

Logaroo: We must have fresh blood everyday to survive!

Ol Higue: We could set up intelligence in the labs...find out whose blood is good and whose is not...

Vetala: Ah but the infrastructure...the resources....do we have enough to accomplish that?

Loud rustling is heard among the rocks.

Asema: You hear something?

Chucu: *Emerging, stammering and a little shy.*) Ah...Ch...ch..chu...Chupacabra...
from Puerto Rico, Peru, Mexico, Uruguay ....at your service!

Chaing: A spy!

Chucu: N...noo! No!

Oba: What are you doing here? You are not one of us!

Chupc: I ...Yes I am (*Points to Jara*) If he is . Then I am!

Chedipe: We have never heard of you!

Chucu: In Spanish my name means....

Cuita and Jara: Bloodsucker?!

Chucu: That's me!

Soucu: *Grinning.*) Yes! The one from the television ! I have heard of you !So
you are real? Pleased to meet you!

Vetala: You are...strictly speaking not one of us.....

Chucu: But I am ! Blood is my business too and I am here to tell you , brothers
and sisters! One must diversify or die! Adapt or snap! Innovate or disappear!
You get my drift?

Oba: I wish you would get to the point. Time going!

Chucu: Blood is life and life is blood. Your solution is animal blood. They are
many. Thousands.
(*Pulls out a little device*) I have a little gadget here that I can trade for something
nominal that will make it perfectly suitable for you....

All: *Look around at each other.*)

Chaing: I need human blood. But if this thing works. Maybe we can copy...

Vetala: Hmmmmmmmm.

Logaroo: Look! Leh we buy the thing yeah?

Oba: But we have so see if it works first....

Chucu: But I am the proof! Look at me!

Chedipe: We need to see the machine work....

Chiang: If go with this gadget...you realize we are condemning humans to die....

All Freeze in horror.

The bell begins to toll. First peal.

All look at each other with deep concern.

Vetala: *Begins to shake again.*)

Second peal.

Oba: *Raises her eyes to the sky.*) It is time.

Third peal.

Chaing: Will we take the machine then?

Fourth peal.

Ol Higue: Do we have a choice?

Fifth peal.

Socu: Of course!

Ol Higue: People have to learn to abstain, refrain!

Logaroo: Suit up! Use rain gear!

Sixth peal.

Asema: And what we going to do in the meantime?!

Oba: Spead the word! About this thing.

Seventh peal.

All : Oba! The name ! What is the name of this dreadful thing?!

Eight peal.

Oba: HIV /AIDS. THE KILLER in the blood!

Ninth peal.

All: HIV /AIDS. THE KILLER in the blood!

Chedipe: *Raises her whip.*)

Tenth peal.

All: *Chanting*) To life! To long life!
Blood is life and life is blood!
Blood is life and life is blood!
Blood is life and life is blood!

Eleventh peal.

All: *Screech in pain and are dragged out by invisible forces until they disappear.*)

Twelfth peal. Silence.

Lights fade to Black.

The End.

Chupacabra –Glossary.

Asema Cuban female blood sucker.
Boops – sound made when something falls from a great height.
Chaing Shih - Chinese male vampire.
Chedipe- Indian woman bloodsucker. Usually depicted as riding a Tiger
Chinee – Chinese
Chucapabra – Latin male. Sucks blood of animals.
Cuitatato – Mexican bloodsucker. Only drinks from children.
Dem – Those
Dougla – Person of mixed race, part East Indian and part African.
Doux-doux mango – very small but extremely sweet type of mango.
Jaracaca- Brazilian male. Drinks breast milk.
Jumbie – ghost/spirit
Logaroo – Male bloodsucker from Haiti and Grenada.
Namaste – Hindu greeting made with both hands clasped and head bowed.
Obayifo - African (Male or female) bloodsucker.
Ol Higue - Guyanese female bloodsucker
Pointer broom- A broom made center stems of the leaf of a coconut tree.
Socuyant - Trinidad female bloodsucker.
Stewps – hissing sound made when one draws air in or lets air out through clenched teeth.
Ting – Thing
Vetala - Indian male vampire .

Yuh – your or you depending on context.

Notes
Though they both drink human blood, a distinction is made between the bloodsucker and the vampire. The vampire can eventually turn the victim into a vampire too, while bloodsuckers generally do not. Bloodsuckers can cause death.

The Massacuraman
A Play in One Act
By Paloma Mohamed
(Winner, Caribbean Secondary School's Drama Festival Best New Play, 2000)

Masacuraman:
" Powerful spirit of the Rivers, he pulls down into
the water at rapids, the boats carrying Pork-knockers into the bush."

A. J Seymour; A Dictionary of Guyanese Folk Characters.

Cast of Characters

1. The Masacuraman
2. Annie - School Girl
3. Ovid - Jeans Husband
4. Neba Jean- Ovid's wife.
5. Old Sam - Village Elder and Annie's Grandfather
6. Edward - Annie's Father
7. Devina - Annie Mother
8. Mr.Joseph - Timber Grant owner and Friend of the Village

The Setting:

The Play is set in the interior region of Guyana. In a wooded part of the Essequibo close to the Timber Grants. There are tall dark trees, abundant wild shrubs, bushes and trees and a powerful river, maybe the Essequibo River that forms a waterway both for the transport of people and logs from the Timber business. The houses of the village are small and clustered together. The village itself is small, maybe 20 families at most. The skyline is dominated by the outline of the Factory
and the huge green heart trees. There are always sounds of chainsaws and men shouting and the hum of birds and insects. The water laps and the engines of boats roar or purr according to their
distance and power. An idyllic country setting, where everyone is happy and content living a simple life.

The Set:

The backdrop of a large factory and huge woods. A long ramp, about 3 ft in width by 12 ft in length runs diagonally from upstage right to downstage left, forming a walkway between the backdrop and the houses. Upstage left the Fronts of two simple houses. They are built on a ramp to give the impression of being above the waterline of the river. Center stage right the sitting and bedroom visible is Annie's Home. There are windows on the back walls of both the sitting room and bedroom. The sitting room is modestly appointed with a small dining table with four chairs its dominant feature. Two settee chairs are in the corner. A door leads of to other parts of the house and to the backyard.

The Time:
Guyana in the 21st century. May -June, the rainy season and final term of school.

The Action:
Scene 1. Jeans birthright.
Scene 2. Jean and Ovid and the plan.
Scene 3. Annie's encounter
Scene 4. The Chickens and the beast
Scene 5. Search for the Beast
Scene 6. Night of the Masacuraman

The Masacuraman
Scene 1

Lights up on the village. It is a soft moonlight night. All the villagers are sitting outside on the ramp liming and gaffing. It is neighbor Jean's birthday.

All; **Singing)** Happy birthday to you, Happy birthday to you , happy birthday dear Jean...
Happy birthday to you...

Jean: Thanks... Thanks a lot... You all make me feel so nice!

Edward: Don't mention Jean. You know youse we girl!

All: Clap in agreement.

Jean: Sorry... things little brown wid we now, and I couldn't fix up some food and cake for you all ...but you know Ovid chain saw down an dat Mr. Joseph won't even lend we the money to buy a new one.

Edward: Why ?

Ovid: He say I gon drink it out ...

Old Sam: He right!

Annie: Grandad!

Devina: Look ...Jean don't worry 'bout dat now girl! We got you covered... (*Calls to Annie*) Annie, go bring out the cook-up and curry chicken that I cook for

Neighba Jean!

Jean: Devi! You all cook fuh me ?!

Edward: Is nothing . You know we mining some fowls? Well they start get coarse now so we cook the first one of the lot for this special occasion your birthday...
Devina: Annie..girl... what you waiting for ? Go quick nah!

Annie walks off.

Old Sam: Devina! You always sending this girl child somewhere in the darkness. I telling you there got things bout the place.

Devi: Papa not again! I tired hearing you stories...

Old Sam: *Calling after Annie)* Annie child wait for you grandfather ! (*To Devina and the others*) You all hard ears. Until something happen you all will not take precautions! I never see any hard ears like this young generation... (*Hurries off after Annie)*

Ovid: Papa! I wonder what he could do with he old self if anything really happen!

Old Sam: I hear dat!

All : Laugh!

Jean: God! That man ears good!

Devi: If it good?! It Lil too good sometimes...if you know what I mean?

Edward: But I invite Mr. Joseph and I ent see he come ?

Jean: So who miss he ?!

Ovid: Don't say that? He is my boss ?

Jean: Look I like to call a spade a spade . That man don't like we. Plus is my birthday at least for one day let me say what I want alright Ovid?! You can't give a gift but at least you could let me say what I want!

Ovid: Is not my fault mek you couldn't get a gift...

Edward: Good! Food!

Annie and Old Sam return with the food. They hand plates to everyone and they all dig into the pots and settle down to eat.

Edward: Ow Devi...everytime I eat you curry I does remember why I married you!

Devi: *Laughing)* Oh?! I thought is for my good looks!
Ovid: But really Devi this food going down real good!

Devi; Thanks ! Well lets take a toast to the birthday girl !

All: To Neighbor Jean ...

Ovid: To love and long life...

Edward: To happiness

Old Sam: To some pickanenny...

Annie: Grandpa!

Old Sam: Is time they get some lil ones to ...

Jean: *Laughing)* Thanks everybody...

Enter Mr. Joseph: And to health and prosperity *(Hands Jean a gift)* Sorry I was late Jean. A problem at the sawmill...

Jean: *Slightly shocked, but grabbing the gift)* This–is for me?

Ovid; *Nudging her)* Jean say thanks !

Jean: Ah.. Yes ... Thanks ... Thank...

Edward: Well we very glad to see you Josey. Sit down and wuk down some of my lovely wife's
culinary delicacies...

Annie: *Laughing)* Daddy ! You definitely swallow a dictionary...

Old Sam: Your father was a very bright boy ! He could go far ...

Edward: Don't start again...

Old Sam: Bright like a bead ...

Annie : *Swinging her foot over the side of the platform)* Really daddy ?

Old Sam: Anita! Put you foot back over right now! I tell you ent good to be swinging yuh foot
over the wata! You will make the work of the Masacuraman easier *(Tugs at*

Annie.)

Annie: But I like to put my feet in the river! It does feel cool and nice like somebody rubbing it ...

Old Sam: Listen to you grandfather. There have all kinda thing in the water. If you have to put yuh foot put it in the daytime when you could see alright ? But for now...

Annie: *Pulls her legs back over)* Ok...ok...

Old Sam: You know how many people get lost in that water? Hundreds !

Devi: Daddy... people does drown. This a riverain area ...

Old Sam: They didn't drown naturally... is Wata Mama and Masacuraman tek them!

Edward: Devi you should know better than to argue with your father ...

Old Sam: Look when the Cinderella capsize you mean to tell me out 12 people none ent save ? None and they was so close to land and at least we know a couple was really good swimmers ?

Ovid: Was the current Old Sam...

Old Sam: Was the Masacuraman... I telling you all, This thing living in this water and it around this timber claim here. I living here since ah born. What I telling you is what I know!

Ovid: You ever see?

Old Sam: I know ?

Ovid: But you never see though?

Old Sam: What you have to see if you know ?!

All: *Laugh)* Old Sam yes...

Old Sam: *Losing his temper)* Laugh...laugh...as if I giving jokes....

Annie: *Hugging him)* Don't worry with them Grandpa... I believe you...

Devi: You better don't listen to too much of this young lady. Cause you know you next thing you can't sleep...

Mr. Joseph: Oh really ? She has that good of an imagination ?

Old Sam: You all call it imagination. I call it for what it is. This Anita born with caul...

Mr. Joseph: Caul ?

Devi: Dad ..

Mr. Joseph: It's ok Devi, I want to know...

Old Sam: Some people born with something like a veil over they face. In Guyana we say is a caul
c-a-u-l! It means that this person is born with the special sensitivity to see, hear and communicate with spirits.

Mr. Joseph: Really ?!

Edward : No not really! That's just what Old Sam say !

Old Sam: That's what everybody in Guyana say. Just that some of us don't want to admit that these things really exist.

Devi: Ok. Whether the girl born with caul or she just imaginative, lets just end this conversation at this hour of the night alright? (*Turns to Anita*) It bed time for you now. Tomorrow is a schooldays...

Annie: *Gets up, half scared)* You all coming or what ?

All: *Laugh)*

Edward: You see what we telling you?! (*Hugs his daughter*) All right frighten Freddy! We commin...

Jean and Ovid rising : No point we staying if everybody else going home.

Mr. Joseph: Ok... but I will sit here a while longer then...there is just something about this moon and this water tonight that is just so enchanting...

Old Sam: Not tonight...I don't advise it , JOSE...

Ovid and Jean : Ok Thanks for everything hear? It was a nice little party. **(They exit stage left to their home across the bank.)**

Edward, Devi, Old Sam and Annie, wave goodnight to Mr. Joseph who remains sitting on the ramp looking out over the water. After a few seconds, a low haunting music is heard. Mr. Joseph looks out closer to the water, the music intensifies and he looks a little closer. Mr. Joseph

rises to his feet and steps back. A huge shadow appears t be rising out of the water. Mr. Joseph steps back, we hear a loud splash. Dead Black out.

Scene 2

About 2 a.m the next morning. The Eerie music continues through out the black out. The Lights rise again on Annie's house. All are asleep. We see a large shadow looming outside Annie's window. As the shadow rises, Annie tosses and turns in her sleep. As the shadow fills the window, Annie screams ! Edward and Devi rush into the room.

Devi: Oh God! Annie.. You ok ...

Edward: It's alright baby we here...

Annie: I ...am sorry to wake you all up...

Devi: I tell you Grandfather not to talk those things by you.

Edward: Annie. You are a big girl now. You going to school and you have intelligence. These things that you Grandfather does talk about is folk tales. Is not real. So you don't have nothing to be afraid of. Is real people that we does have to look out for in this life . NO spirit and things like that . Alright ?

Annie: *Nods)*

Devi: *Hugging the Girl)* So...you just say your prayers and go to sleep ok. *(Kisses her forehead)*

Annie: *Grabbing her mothers neck)* Mommy...you all stay with me till I go to sleep... please ?..

Edward and Dev get into the bed on either side of Annie. Annie soon falls asleep. Edward and Devi tip toe lightly out of the room. But as Devi passes the window she shivers.)

Edward: *Whispers)* What ?

Devi: Just got a chill passing here ...

Edward: Oh God! Not you too ! Look nothing there (*Pulls back the blind to reveal the bedroom window wide open.)* What .. The .. (*Turns to Devi...)* You left this window open ?!

Devi: No... I close it before we went to the party Edward...

64

Edward: You sure ?

Devi: Yes.. And I check it again after we tuck her in tonight...

Edward: *Closing the window)* Ok... Must be Annie open it to get some breeze. You must remind me to tell her she mustn't do that. You never know when thief roaming about.... *(They turn off the light and Exit.)*

In the darkness we hear the sounds of footsteps in the distance and something heavy being dragged. After a while we see a light bobbing up and down. As the lights come nearer we hear urgent voices.

Jean : Look hurry up man ! Hurry up...

Ovid: I hurrying. But dis thing heavy yuh know....

Light up to reveal Jean carrying a Lamp and Ovid is pulling a large fishing seine. It is almost dawn.

Jean: I don't want nobody to see me doing this ...

Ovid: So what ? Everybody does catch fish...

Jean: Look shut up hear! Just shut up! I didn't marry no fisher man! I marry a businessman, a timberman. Is you with your carelessness, cause all this! Imagine my birthday and you couldn't even buy me a gift ?!

Ovid: Is not my fault the chain saw burn...Jean..

Jean: Make... them show off Devi and she husband had to feed we on my birthday...

Ovid: That ent nutting. That's how we in this village does live.

Jean: You all don't have no shame! Ovid. It embarrassing....If you can't feed yourself, if you can't look after you home, if you can't buy nice things for you wife it embarrassing!

Ovid: Maybe fuh you! Everybody does go through a bad patch. People understand...

Jean: Well I tired of people sorrying fuh me ok.. If you don't do something fast I will be outa here ! You understand ? Out of here ! *(She put down the lamp and storms off)*

65

Ovid: Casts his seine) Huh! I should never marry a girl who was not from here. She not content...

Ovid: Pulls in his seine shakes it nothing. Sucks his teeth.) Dis river bare. I never see this river so bare.... *(Throws the seine again. Pulls in again. Nothing.)* Is like nothing I do can't come to
success. Can't cut wood, can't catch fish ...can't make my wife happy, can't make children...
(Casts the seine again) Ow lord... just one load for today. To keep Jean happy ad buy some rations...just one load eh? *(Pulls the seine nothing)*

The lights grow brighter indicating day clean. Jean stands watching him from a distance shaking her head while all this is going on. She exits into the house and returns with a cup of tea. She crosses to Ovid and sits down on the ramp beside him. She offers the tea quietly to him.

Jean: Gently) I know you trying. I know you trying really hard...

Ovid: Doesn't answer, but tosses the seine again)

Jean: Stop a Lil bit an' listen to me. I got an idea.... *(Tugs at his hand)*

Ovid: Pulls in the seine again. A single fish plops out. He picks it up and puts it in his pail in desperation.)

In the distance we hear the voices of Annie and Devi.

Devi: Annie! Don't live in the bathroom girl!

Annie: Coming Ma!

Devi: You will be late fuh school !

Annie: Coming!

Jean: You hear ...people getting ready to come out. Put up the seine Ovid...before people see.

Ovid: Pulls in the seine and sits.)

Jean; Hands him the tea.)

Ovid: Takes it quietly and sips)

Jean: Puts her head on his shoulder lovingly.) You know...I been thinking. I know of a way to get some money quick so you could get back you saw and start back

66

working the timber grant ...

Ovid: Really ?

Jean: Yes...But if I tell you ... you might vex with me...
Ovid: Why ?

Jean: Because ...is not something too nice...

Ovid: Then why you tellin' me?

Jean: Because ...I can't think of nothing else ! But if you don't want to hear ....

Enter Edward on the way to work.

Edward: Jean , Ovid! You all early man...

Jean: Just tekking some morning breeze...

Edward: Enjoy it! I hustling to work here! Late ! Annie keep us up a bit last night .. (*Rushes off.*)

Jean: Damn stupid country people. And they raising the child just so superstitious like them.

Ovid: Annie is a very intelligent child!

Jean: Look don't eat off my head alright! I know is you godchild and she could do no wrong.

Ovid: Look leave Annie out of this ok!

Jean: Look Ovid. You know I love that child. I love her like she is my own. So calm down...

Ovid : Sips his tea)

Jean: Is silent. Throwing pebbles into the water.)

Ovid: So what we going to do ?

Jean: You will be the Masacuraman..

Ovid: *Choking on his tea)* What?!

Jean: Yes. This village believe in that stupidness. They will buy it. And nobody will suspect is you.

Ovid: But how that will make us money ? You planning to sell me to the zoo ?!

Jean: The Masacuraman will start to thief chickens. Everybody chickens and then we get enough money for you to buy back you chainsaw, we stop. And everybody happy!

Ovid: Jean! I can't do that ?! These people is friends of mine... some a dem is family ...

Jean: A few chickens ent gon kill them...but it might kill we...

Ovid: Jean look...I can't do that alright. It wrong.

Jean: *Rising angry)* Ok! *(Flouncing off)* Just be prepared to sleep on the floor tonight!

Dead Black Out.

Scene 3

The next evening. Annie is going down to the river with a bucket of clothes. She goes down to the waters edge and washes. As she washes the strange eerie sound of music is heard very low in the background. The light grow dim ever so imperceptibly. Suddenly a shadow begins to emerge from the river. Annie sees it and rises from her washing staring almost transfixed. Then she begins to walk slowly out into the water. Her arms outstretched. The shadow also opens its arms as if to receive her. The music grows louder and louder. As Annie jumps into the water a loud splash is heard. As the lights grow brighter and the music diminishes we see Mr. Joseph with the lifeless body of Annie emerging from the river. He lays her on the river bank and attempts to giver her resuscitation.

Enter Jean: Aye ! Joseph! Is what you doing to Annie!?

Joseph: Ignoring her and continues to pump Annie's stomach)

Jean Raising an Alarm: Devi! Eddie! Old Sam ! Al yuh come see what this man doing to Annie! I catch he read handed! Everybody you all come! Joseph holding down we Annie!

Joseph: Continues to give the girl mouth to mouth.)

Annie: begins to cough)

Joseph: That's it! That's my girl...Come on Annie...come on...

The others arrive)

Jean: I tell you all. I see! With me own eyes I see. This man holding down Annie on the beach...

Devi : Annie...what happened ?

Annie: I...don't know...Mammy...

Edward : Joseph ...?!

Joseph: Eddie I swear she was going to drown...I was saving her ...

Jean: Lie! Annie is a good swimmer! Nobody don't drown in the shallow . shallow water ! He had she hold down kissing she. An if I didn't come I don't know what else he would do to she! You all ought to thank me....

Edward: *Picks Annie up and takes her back to the house)* Devi and Old Sam follow. So does Mr. Joseph.

Jean: Calling after them) Joseph is a devil! You all going to see! (*Walks off in the direction of her house.)*

At Annie House. Devi Takes Annie and puts her to bed. The men are left outside talking.

Joseph: Look Eddie, I know it sound funny, but when Annie recovers you can ask her. This is like my own child man! I saved her from drowning! You got to believe me...

Eddie: My daughter is a good swimmer. That is shallow water...

Joseph: Yes... I know but she was walking out to the deep, like if she was in a trance !

Eddie: Oh yes? So what you was doing down these parts? You living in the rich side across the river what you was doing down here now ?

Joseph: I was coming to have a word with old Sam about something I thought I saw the other night in the river ..

Eddie: Nonsense! I'm going to get to the bottom of this! And if she say you so much as laid a finger on her! I don't care how much big shot you is ! I will hunt you down like a hungry tiger and I will personally rip you apart hip from shoulder!

69

Old Sam: Edward! This is no way to treat someone who just give you back your daughter!

Eddie: Listen old man. You stay out of this! Just stay out of this !!

Old Sam: That woman Jean is a trouble maker! You can't accuse this man before you know the real story! I tired tell you all don't send Annie down by the river. Water spirits going to fall in love wid her...

Edward: You mad ! Mad as hell! This is my house and I could accuse whoever I want ! Annie is my daughter and I could accuse who ever I want ! (*walks over to Joseph*) You better pray that this story you giving is true. Otherwise is me an you!   (*He storms out of the room*)

Joseph: *Exit into the night without a word.)*

Old Sam : *Hurries after him)* You said you was coming to see me Josie...

Joseph : Forget it! I got to get out of these wet clothes...

Old Sam: Boy! Listen to me ! I know you hurt and you angry. But I want to thank you for saving my Little Annie. I know you save she and whatever the reason you was down by that river tonight was Godsend you.

Joseph: *Sighs long and hard)* It was so funny....one minute she was there beating the clothes with that little stick she uses. I stood there watching her...so young and the river and all this greenery surrounding her. And I thought how wonderful to be so young and carefree again...So I just stopped walking for a moment , just to watch her...it was innocent really... I was really only watching her ...

Old Sam: I believe you...and what you see while you was watching her ?

Joseph: She stopped suddenly. Very suddenly and stood up bone straight.

Old Sam:; She looked like she was looking at something ?

Joseph: Yes...Yes..but I swear there was nothing there...

Old Sam: So you think...

Joseph: And then she just started to walk out into the river. She was walking dead straight with her arms outstretched like if she was greeting somebody. Just like that until the water was almost to her waist then I thought something is really wrong and I jumped in and tried to stop her. But she fought me Old Sam. She really fought me as if she had the strength of ten men. And the current,

70

it grew so powerful, that for a moment I thought it was all over...for her and for me. (*Exhales deeply*) I know it sounds funny. But that's what happened...really...

Old Sam: Masacuraman.

Joseph: What?

Old Sam: For some reason he come back here...

Joseph: Come back ? It was here before?

Old Sam: You too young . You wouldn't know. But you father old Joe. He would know and you Grandfather. (*Sits down)* Was a time when this thing used to terrorize this village. People used to see a shirt hairy creature coming out of the water in the night. People used to drown by the dozens, big-big boats overturn for no reason, and death and death and death all around.

Joseph: What happened ?

Old Sam: Was an old Amerindian man named Aloucious, that they call. Was that man that was able to identify what was going on. It was a water spirit, a creature they called the Masacuraman.
He is said to be part man, part beast, that's why he so hairy and strong. That's why he likes blood.

But is a long time since he ain't come by this village. Aloucious did fix that. But he coming back now..he coming back now...I wonder what could be the meaning of that ?!

Dead Black Out.

Scene 4

Early the next morning loud screams are heard from Annie's house. Devi is running around screaming hysterically.

Devi: Oh my God! Oh my God Al yuh come ! Al yuh come ! Eddie oh God Eddie!

Enter Eddie with his towel around him) Devi ?! What goin' on...

Devi: *Pointing to the back of the house where the chickens are.)* They got blood everywhere Eddie! I never see so much blood...

Edward rushes around to the house. He comes back with his hand dripping with

71

blood.) Jeeesus! The chickens...the chickens...

Enter Old Sam: What happen to the chickens ?

Devi: Look like something eat them Pa!

Old Sam: *Hurries around to the back. Edward follows him.)*

Enter Annie: Ma? Pa?

Devi: Annie. Don't come out here baby! *(Takes her back into the house)* Come inside...

Edward : *Calling over the bank)* Ovid! Aye Ovid!

Ovid: *Comes out rubbing his eyes)* What ?!

Edward: Come see this !

Ovid: *Ambles over. Then he flies back to the front of the house.)* God! Oh God! (*He begins to throw up)*

Edward: Devi! Pass a bucket. We gon have to wash down this whole place!

Devi: Comes out with a bucket. Sees Ovid puking. Goes back in and hands him a bucket too)

Ovid: *Takes it)* Sorry (*Goes down to the river. Fills it and comes back. Washes away his vomit.)*

Old Sam and Edward come into the sitting room after a while.)

Edward sitting with his hands on his head.) Every single chicken I raise.. Old Sam. Is every single chicken this thing eat! Not one ent get save! Not one!

Old Sam: I still think is the work of a thief ...

Edward: No thief coulda thief 50 chicken and nobody ent hear . The pen right under we bedroom window! And no thief woulda massacre the birds like that, and spill they blood all over the place ...
That was some wild animal or beast...

Ovid: *Sits there very quiet)*

Old Sam: No wild beast could fly that latch.

72

Edward: Them things intelligent ...

Old Sam: Not that latch...

Edward: Maybe Annie left the latch open when she went to feed the birds last night...

Ovid: Softly) Masacuraman

Edward: What ?

Ovid : Masacuraman ...

Edward: There is nothing like a Masacuraman! This got to be the work of a Jaguar or a Tiger...! And the next thing is when they finish with the animals and the birds they coming for the humans! (Rises)Ovid get the men together...this is serious business! Old Sam you still got that shot gun ?

Old Sam: Nods absentmindedly)

Edward: I gon need it !

Ovid: Is still sitting there)

Edward: Ovid! You in a trance! Go tell the other men we got a wild animal on the prowl. Let them bring any weapon they have ! Go ! Now!

Ovid; Wanders off still in a daze.

Devi: Brings Old Sam's gun and hands it to Edward) You all be careful ok. (She also hands him
some food in a little leather bag.) You food. Enough for you and Ovid and two other people. You all be careful ... (She gives him a quick hug.)

Edward: Old Sam, you stay here.

Old Sam : Indignantly) When I was catching Tiger you didn't even dream to born!

Edward:) You will slow us up.

Old Sam: I will slow you up?! I will slow you up !

Edward: Takes his stuff and strides out)

Old Sam: You will hear about me!! Old Man don't run but he does ketch!

Devi: Pa! Don't fret...You could stay here and protect Annie and me.

Old Sam: *Preoccupied)* Hmmmmm...I hope this old man still alive... *(Exits the house)*

Devi: Pa where you going ? Edward say for you to stay here ?

Old Sam: Tell Edward I say my father dead before he born! You keep Annie in this house you hear me. At all costs, watch she like a hawk. I think I know exactly what going on here ! *(Exits)*

Dead Black Out.

Scene 5

One week later. Ovid, Mr. Joseph & Edward are returning to Annie's house. Old Sam is sitting on a short stool or box at the front door with a basket of herbs.

Old Sam: *Chuckling to himself)* So you all ent ketch dis tiger yet ?

The men pass him and go into the house.)

Edward: You have to excuse him. He really getting old now...

Joseph: He's a jolly old boy. You gotta like the man.

Ovid: Look.... Eddie. I don't mean to cause no problems with you. But is a whole week now the whole village searching for this beast and nobody ent so much as see a Track.

Edward: But the same things happening to everybody one by one Ovid! Everybody ! There got to be some explanation!

Ovid: Masacuraman...

Old Sam: *From the door)* Masacuraman don't use animal blood Ovid. They feed only on human blood...

Ovid: What ?!

Old Sam: *Entering the room)* Plus the Masacuraman is a river creature. He don't strike unless a thing is in the river or very near the river... So he uses his eyes to

74

hypnotize his victims and lead them to the river. He is only powerful in the water!

Joseph: That's why ...

Old Sam: *Motions to him to shush)*

Ovid: Well whatever it is... Is a whole week now that I out every night and leaving my nice young wife alone.

Edward: But Devi invite Jean to come sleep here and she refuse...

Ovid: She like to stay in she own place, but after tonight Edward, I can't leave my wife alone anymore ok...I sorry.
Joseph: Eddie, the man has a point...this can't go on forever...

Edward: so what you all saying? Call off the search ?!

Joseph: I think so...

Edward: Something slaughtering all the chickens in this village and you all just going to leave it like that ? Old Mr. Persaud lost his whole pen. Miss. Agard loss 20, and the Mongroo's farm loss about 100 in the space of a week! Apart from the hundreds of thousands of dollars involved ? You all don want to know what going on ?! You don't want to know ?

Joseph: Yes... we want to know but life has to go on.

Ovid: Yes...people have they life to live...

Edward: *Reluctantly)* Well if you all want to stop... you can stop but I will never back off. I going to keep vigil until this problem solve...

Old Sam: Hmmmmmmm. (*Walking around shaking his pot of herbs*)

Ovid and Joseph rise to leave.

Joseph: So what's in the pot Old Sam ?

Old Sam: Aloucious Brew..

Joseph: Really ?

Old Sam: Masacuraman in de village. Confirmed...

Ovid : What ?!

75

Joseph: Confirmed old Man ?

Old Sam: Yes...

Joseph: But how ?

Old Sam: People see it...

Ovid: You sure old Sam...

Old Sam: And it have a mission. A urgent mission that's why he come now....

Edward: I thought you say, that this thing happening in the village have nothing to do with this...this ridiculous Masacuraman ?! Now you saying something else.!!

Old Sam: I said he don't eat chicken. I said is human blood he uses. So is not he that doing the chicken thing. That's what ah said. I old but I ent senile yet!

Joseph: So why he come back this time Old Sam ? What he want...

Old Sam: A wife ?!

Joseph: What ?!

Ovid: Look ! Don't be crazy now old Sam!

Old Sam: Call me what you may. Masacuraman got to pass on his spirit to a son. He need a human female. That's why he come.

Joseph: Oh my God! Sam...I...surely It can't be what I am thinking...!!

Ovid: *Exiting hurriedly)* Look this whole thing getting crazy! I t getting dark and I going home to my wife! See you all tomorrow!

Joseph: *Sits down again)* What can we do...

Old Sam: Secure the house...

Edward: Wait! Wait! This fictitious person want the female from in hay ?

Old Sam: *Nods. Still busy with his bouquet)*

Edward: Not Devi ?!

Old Sam: She done mek a child. He got to have a woman who womb is clean...

76

Joseph : *In horror)* Annie...

Edward: The Masacuraman coming for my little twelve year old daughter Annie? To make a baby Masacuraman fuh he ? (*Laughs. Then stops suddenly.*) Well hear what I have to tell the two of you ! I don't know what sick plot that you all working out between you all. But is a long time I watching you Joseph wid my daughter. I tell you once and I tell you twice ...anything happen to Annie...
Old Sam : Shut up Edward! You is a highly intelligent man but you so ignorant ! That is the trouble with people these days. You concentrate so much on other things that you lose touch with spirit. And sometimes they right here talking to we and we so busy we don't pay attention. The Masacuraman is a spirit. An old, old water spirit. Last time he come here was because Joseph father did start to log out this land and pollute the river, which is the Masacuraman domain. Aloucious the old Amerindian Piaiman fix dat. The Masacuraman went to other places. But now he come back here.

Now you could doubt me if you want. But the price that you would have to pay for that will be too high for me to bear otherwise I would just leave you in you ignorance. But old people say... know better do better. (*Walks out into the yard)* So I just going to do better! And if you can't find some way to help, just stay outta my damn way!

Dead Black Out

Scene 6

That same night. Old Sam and Mr. Joseph are keeping vigil outside the door of Annie's House. Edward is sitting in a chair in the living room trying to stay awake. The shotgun is in his lap. As the clock strikes midnight a strange howling sound is heard. It is a sound that a tornado might make as it crosses water. Old Sam hears it and sits very still. No one else hears it. In her room Annie sleeps soundly.

Across the way a figure creeps out of Jeans house. The figure is wearing dark garments and is masked so that we cannot detect who or what it is. The figure slinks across the stage and out of sight as the howling sounds grow louder.

Old Sam gets up. Standing very quietly he listens and looks out into the night.

77

Old Sam: Lord this is a hellish night tonight! Dear God if I never do anything successful ...before I close me eye. Let me do this right tonight!

The howling sound grows stronger. Inside, Eddie paces the floor. A shadow looms at the window of Annie's room. She begins to toss for a while. Then the voice of her mother is heard calling her.

Devi's Voice) Annie! Come outside Annie! I need you Annie! Don't be afraid Annie. I won't hurt you Annie! It's me Mommy!

Annie: In a Trance gets out of bed and goes to the window. It is already swinging open.)

Devi's voice: Come out Annie! Come out to me...Through the window Annie, down to the water Annie come to Mommy!

Annie : Still in a trance like state climbs through the window and heads for the water her arms outstretched, walking very slowly.)

From the river the figure of a huge hairy man with bushy hair in which there are caught snakes. His arms reach out of the water beckoning to Annie. We recognize that it is from this figure that Devi's voice is coming. It continues to beckon and call to the girl and Annie continues to go to the water.

In the sitting room Edward is acing faster. He decides to check on Annie. Pushes open the door and finds that she is not there. He calls Annie! Annie!

Devi's Voice: Come Quickly Annie! Come quick! Time is passing! Come quick....

Edward moves to the open bedroom window but he cannot see his daughter. He checks all over the house for her. Then he bursts outside to Old Sam.

Edward: She's gone...

Old Sam: Shaking Joseph awake : Dear God.. Protect us...

Edward: I brought the shot gun... and a silver bullet...just in case...

Old Sam: Nods . They all head off hurriedly towards the water.)

As Annie nears the waters edge the figure that had left Jeans house minutes before returns hurriedly heading for Jeans house. But there is a huge crocus bag full of something on the figures shoulders. This bag is obviously heavy. As the figure approaches the bank Annie come into it's line of sight.

The figure stops short. Annie continues to follow the instructions of the voice and to approach the Masacuraman. The figure carrying the bag follows Annie's line of sight and sees the Masacuraman. It lets out a loud scream! It drops the bag it has been carrying and screams.

Jean: Ahhhhhhhhhhh! Masacuraman! Somebody! Anybody help! Annie Oh God! Oh God! Yeah though I walkthroughthe valley of the shadow of death.... (*She tries to hold Annie back.*)

Jean: Oh God! Help somebody! Somebody! Annie ! Stop Annie!

Enter Old Sam, Joseph and Edward running.

Old Sam: Annie! Don't look at his eyes Annie! Don't look! And don't listen either . Is not your mother calling you . Is not you mother. This creature imitating her to trap you!

Enter Devi: Annie! Annie! Stop !

Annie : Hears her mothers voice and stops momentarily as if confused)

The Masacuraman begins to call in another females voice that of Annie's Grandmother.)
Devi: *Upon hearing the other voice)* Mammy ?! Is that you Mammy ?

Old Sam: Oh God...Don't listen Sammy Boy!

Jean: Is holding on to the girl but she is having a hard time holding her .

Old Sam: Rushes forward and throws his basket of bushes into the water.)

At the same time Jean rushes forward.) Is somebody you want ? Take me then! Take me...leave my God daughter take me...

The Masacuraman grabs for her and she disappears from view under the water.

Edward rushes forward and grabs Annie out of the water.

Joseph: *Tries to help Jean)* Jean !

Old Sam: Don't go in that water Joseph... you can't save her !

Joseph: *Dives into the water.)*

Devi: *Shouting)* Ovid! Oh God! Ovid Jean gone down in de water ...

Ovid : *Comes rushing out of the house rubbing his eyes)* Whaa...at?!

Devi: *Hugging on to him.)* Jean...gone down Ovid..she gone down...

Ovid: But ...no! Jean in she bed Devi...she ...

Old Sam: Masacuraman...she gone down...

Ovid: *Sinks to the floor his head in his hands)* No...no! Not my Jean....NO!

Joseph: Surfaces with Jeans lifeless body in his arms. He gives her mouth to mouth and pumps her chest as the others pray silently.)

Old Sam: Stands vigil next to Annie and Edward and come upon the bag that Jean dropped.

At this same time Jean opens her eyes and begins to cough.

Old Sam: *Picking up the bag and tumbling out the contents)* Old Man don't run but he does ketch! So was you thieving the chickens ent Jean ?

Jean: Laughs ghoulishly. Sits bolt upright with unseeing eyes. Grabs Ovid and plunges right back into the water. A Loud splash is heard and the howling of the wind intensifies as the lights turn to dead black.

The End

Massacuraman- Glossary

Alyuh – All of you. Everyone.
Caul – Membrane over newborns face. Said to enable those born with it to see spirits.
Dat- That
Ent – Don't or won't depending on context.
Ent nutting – It's nothing
Gon – Going to/ will
Lil – little
Massacuraman- Powerful spirit of the rivers of Guyana. He pulls boats down into the water at rapids.
Mek – Make
Neighba/Neba – Neighbor
Nutting – Nothing
Piaiman – Amerindian bush doctor. Shaman
Pickanenny – Children /offspring
Sorrying – Being sorry or becoming sorry for someone
Stupidness – Great stupidity
Tek- Take
Things brown – things are hard
Timberman – someone who works as a logger.
Wata – Water
Wid – With
Work down / wuk down – to imbibe / drink and eat heartily
Youse – You do/ usually you
Yuh- You

Sukanti
A Play in One Act
By Paloma Mohamed.

Sukanti – Completely invisible male or female evil spirit which possesses people especially young girls who wear their hair loose at night. Also attacks children. Victims pine away until death unless the spirit is exorcised by a Muslim or Hindu priest.

Characters (In order of appearance)

1.Bap : Old Grandfather of Kishna and Gitangili. Also known as Bamsingh. Staunch Hindu.
2.Shaira Khan: Next Door neighbor. Muslim. In late 50's. Wife of Yusuf.
3.Yusuf Khan: Next Door neighbor. Well to do. Early 60's. Husband of Shaira.
4. Gitangili Bamsingh: Also called Gita and Geet. Age 17. Bap's granddaughter.
5. Kishna: Also called Kish. 24. Bap's grandson. Medical student.
6. Ayube Khan: Shaira and Yusuf's son. Strong and strikingly handsome. Has slight downs syndrome.
7. Panditji: The Pandit. Staunch Hindu.
8.Rajiv Parasad: Panditji's son. Age 22.
9. Padma: Panditji's wife. Appears but does not speak.
10. Extras at funeral.

The Setting: Suburbs of Georgetown, Guyana, maybe Prashad Nagar or Bel Air Springs. Sometime in the late 1990's. The area is not opulent but it is decent. Houses are well spaced. There are biggish yards, with trees and flower plants. Some of them have Hindu shrines and *jandi's*[1] in the front yard. There are three houses visible against the background of an imposing Hindu temple. One the home of Pandit "Panditji"[2] is bigger than the others and has numerous and more colorful flags in the front yard. The sitting room and front yard of Panditji's house are visible. This house is located left of center. The second house located downstage right is smaller than Panditji's's house but bigger and fancier than the third house at center stage. This is the home of the Yusuf Khan's. Only the frontage of the house, fence and front yard are visible. At center stage is the house of the Bamsingh's. This is a humble and much smaller space, but clean and well kept. The sitting room and a small veranda are visible.

The Set:
Panditji's House : Action takes place in sitting room and yard only. Opulent and full of religious and old Hindu artifacts. There are two other active exits. One at right to upper flat and bedrooms, one at left to kitchen and other rooms in house.

Bamsingh's House : Simple but well appointed. A single picture of Lord Shiva on the wall , over the passage way to the bedrooms. Action only in yard, veranda and sitting room. A hammock is slung across veranda sometimes. Two exits to others parts of the house are active. Door at stage left is exit to kitchen and back door. Door off center is exit to bedrooms.

The Action: The play takes place over eight months.

Scene 1

Saturday afternoon, just after dusk. Lights up on Bamsingh's house. BAP Bamsingh is entertaining Shaira and Yusuf. Gitangili Bamsingh is in the passageway and can be seen peeping around the corner every now and then as the adult conversation takes place.

Yusuf: So...that is the proposition!

Bap: *Is silent.)*

Shaira: Yes! That is it!

Yusuf: Is a good opportunity Bap !

Bap: *Still silent.)*

Shaira: A very good opportunity!

Bap: A very good opportunity eh? Fuh who?!

Yusuf: Well...

Shaira: For Gitangili!

Bap: True?

Shaira: Ayube is we only child. Bap...we have....

Yusuf: Shaira! Let me talk! You not putting it right. (*Takes a deep breath*) Look Bap, we know you is a respectable man who raise your grandchildren like if they was your own children.

Bap: *Folds his legs under him and settles deeper into the chair)* Gita!?

Gita: *Is startled behind the door)* Yes! Yes...Bap?

84

Bap: Gita come bring some drink for these people dem.

Gita: *Emerges rolls her eyes*) Yes, Bap.

Bap: Good. (*To Yusuf*) Yuh 'tory sound long. We go wet *abe*[3] throat and *tek am in*[4].

Yusuf: (*Sheepishly*) Thanks Bap. I was saying that we know you is a respectable family just like *awe*. That is why we come to you with this *preposition*[5]. You from the old tradition. Yuh know how to do things proper.

Bap: *Sighs.*)

Yusuf: Ayube is we only child so when I gone he go get all my money.

Enter Gita with the drinks. She serves Bap first then serves Yusuf and then Shaira.

Shaira: Whoever marry my Ayube will be a lucky, lucky girl!

Yusuf: *Shooting Shaira a look.*)

Bap: Ok. *Beti*[6]

Gita retreats to the bedrooms.

Shaira: *Taking a sip*) Lovely child!

Yusuf: Ayube and Gita...they both of them of age...

Shaira: Before dem get themself in trouble Bap!

Yusuf: Yes! True!

Bap: Alright. I have a question.

Yusuf: Yes?

Bap: I look like a blasted ass to you all ?!

Yusuf: Bap!

Bap: Look get you *rass*[7] out me house you hear, before I do something *jabberjasty*[8]*!*

Shaira: We come here in peace! No need to insult we!

Bap: *You* come ya[9] fuh insult *awe* dis! Yuh tink seh cause me house flat and you own high me go tek me one grain granddaughter and marry am off to you *phagala*[10] son?!

Shaira: What happen?! He is a human being like everybody else! You grandchildren ent better than my son!

Bap: *Sucks his teeth loudly.*)

Shaira: Look Yusuf, leh we go ! This *babu* [11] here ain't worth a cent of we money!

Bap: You could talk 'bout babu?! When you sell your son fo' get riches?! Now you want burden me poor little Gita with dat *karma* [12]? Yuh tink seh me stupid? Me don't know 'bout these things them?

Yusuf: Sell? We didn't sell....

Bap: You might want discuss it with yuh wife, not with me. I sorry fuh you all and for Ayube. But I can't marry Gita to he.

Shaira: Yuh go sorry! Was a good offer! Yuh go see who else go want she!

Bap: That ent concern ayo![13]

Yusuf: Ok. We going. But if you change your mind...

Bap: Nah bother. Gita deserve better!

Shaira: Better?! Better than who?! *Ayo dese* blood done taint *areddy*[14]! You think I don't know why you leff Berbice come live here ?

Yusuf : *Grabs her and pulls her towards the door)* Shaira! Enough! Come home!

Shaira: *Over her shoulder*) Playing you better than everybody else?!!

Yusuf and Shaira exit in a huff.

A Jumbie Bird screeches into the night.

Bap: *Sits deep in thought.*)

Gita: *Comes out, sees him and gives Bap a hug*) Thanks Bap...

Bap: Wha da fuh? [15]

Geeta: *Catching herself*) Ah....I....I just love you Bap! (*Starts clearing the glasses.*)

Bap: *Grunts, walks out to the verandah and lets down his hammock. He settles into a deep reverie as he rocks.*)

Enter Kishna.

Kishna: Night Bap!

Bap: Night Kishna Bamsingh!

The phone rings. Kishna hurries to answer but Bap stops him.

Bap: Yuh just come from studying. Sit down. Rest yuh foot! Let yuh sister gi[16] you food *bhai*[17]!

Kishna : *Still tries to get to the phone but Bap pulls him down into the hammock*) Siddown! Phone is distraction! Remember what important!

Kishna: *Sighs but gives in to his grandfather.*

Gita: *Gets the phone .)*

Kishna: *Mimes the question "is it for me?")*

Gita: *Mimes back "you wish"! Says,)* Is for Bap!

Bap: *Rises, shuffles to the phone*) This is Bamsingh! (*Listens for a while then sighs loudly*) Hai Krishna! Me ah come now! (*Hangs up. Calls to Gita*) Gita! Bring me slippa dem! (*To Kishna*) After you eat, come down the road meet be by Panditji.

Kishna: Bap! I am tired ....

Bap: And bring yuh sista when you come. (*To Gita, as she brings his slippers*) Put on something nice, hear? (*Puts on the slippers*) And remember to tie up your hair ! *Nah mek*[18] *Sukhanti*[19] come pon you like Black miss Mavis daughta up the road! (*Hurries up the road.*)

Kishna: *Sucking his teeth loudly as soon as the old man is out of earshot*) Sukhanti! Where Bap does get these ideas from, only he know!

Gita: *Emerging with food on a small plastic tray*) He know what he saying.

Kish: Look ! I am a man of science, you hear? I don't believe nothing that I can't dissect in a lab!

Gita: Everything can't dissect boy!

Kish: Everything that is not your imagination can!

Gita: Look boy! Eat.

Kish: I can't deal with Panditji at this hour of the night! Too much a rule and regulation! Tek off you shoe, plait your foot, wash off the *renk* [20]....

Gita: Eat. Look, I make your favorite *aloo parata*[21] and *Hassar* curry today!

Kishna: *Laughs and gives her a small pinch on the cheek*) You know how to get me over good!

Gita: *Giggles*) Hurry up fast and then we can go!

Kishna: *Teasing her*) Why you *so* hurry?

Gita: Me ?

Kish: *Laughing*) Good. This food too sweet to hurry. I got to take one small mouthful at a time....

Gita: *Looks over at the next yard, sees something that causes her to shiver suddenly*. **She exits into the house.**

Kishna: *Looks after Gita, then into the next yard.*)

Ayube: *Emerges from the shadows with a flower in his hand.*)

Kishna: Hi Ayube!

Ayube: *Offers the flower to Kishna)* Give Geeeeeeta.! (*Smiles happily.*)

Kishna: *Hesitates for a minute and then takes the flower)* Thanks.

Black Out.

Scene 2

Two weeks later at Bap's house. Lights up to the sound of the Jumbie bird screeching. Bap is lying on the hammock groaning loudly. Gita is rubbing his head with mentholated spirits. Kishna is trying to make him comfortable.

Bap: No! No hospital Kish. Is jus' a little *nara*[22]. You look after Bap. Me want *you* tek care ah me!

Kishna: But I am not a Doctor yet....you need....

Bap: Three year more or five year more...what difference it go make? *You* ah *me* docta!

Kish: Bap ! Look ! You could get me In trouble. If anything happen to you they could say is my fault....I never took you to get proper care.....

Bap: Hospital Docta *nah*[23] fix dis, Bhai! (*Lets out another loud groan.*)

Gita: You see! I tell you not to spend every day for the whole two weeks at Savitri funeral *yag*[24]. Youse an old man! It was too much!

Bap: You want Panditji people dem to say we don't know bout nothing proper? Now that Rajiv is a widower? You think I could take dat risk and not be there all the time in this time of sorrow?

Kish: Bap. Gita is right. You overdid it. Plus you don't like to listen to advice.

Bap: *Sucks his teeth and then immediately bursts into a fit of coughing.*)

Gita: Bap?

Bap: *Weakly)* Geet....go bring me *book* Beti.

89

Gita goes inside for the book.

Bap: *Grasps Kishna's hand tightly and pulls him toward him)* Meh hear *Mush-shi-ki-re*[25] calling five night in a row now.... You go take good care of you sister ?

Kish: Bap...look.......

Bap: *Coughs again and continues)* And promise me you go *get you docta paper*[26]....

Kish: *Nods.)*

Bap: *Looking around suspiciously)* And promise me, that you never go marry yuh sister to dem *chamar*[27] dem!

Kish: *Surprised) Who?*

Bap: Ayube.

Enter Gita with the book , a very worn copy of the *Bhagvadgita*[28]

Bap : *Falls silent.)*

Gita: *Offers the book to Bap.)*

Bap: *Signals to Kish to take it from his sister.)*

Kish: *Hesitates.)*

Bap: *Goes into a fit of coughing.)*

Kish: *Takes the book.)*

Bap: Me know when me woulda dead from the day I come into dis world here. (*Breathes deeply*) My Bap tell me seh Pandit read and tell him, they woulda kill me for my riches (*Gasps again.*)

Gita: Bap!

Kish: Get some water!

Gita goes for the water.

Bap: *Motions to the book)* Read it everyday *Beta*[29]. It will never lead you wrong (*Coughs grabs Kish's hand*) Is dem people next door bring this on me now! They covet me riches dem!

90

Kish: *Feeling Bap's forehead*) What riches ?! We don't have no money Bap!

Bap: Flesh worth more than diamond....

Enter Gita with the water.
She tries to make Bap drink but he gurgles and spits the water out at her.

The lights grow very dim. The Jumbie bird screeches again. Faint sitar music is heard. Hindu death music begins to waft in and out of earshot in half made stanzas as if being received by bad reception.

The lights grow dimmer. Music grows louder.

Kish: Bap! Oh God Bap! (*To Gita*) Call the ambulance....

Gita: *Screams*) Baaaaaaap!

Ayube rushes over from next door.

Kish: Bap! You can't die now! I wouldn't know what to do ....

Shaira and Yusuf emerge from next door.

Yusuf: Come! I can tek him to the hospital in my car!

Bap makes a loud gurgling sound sits up straight. Then stands up straight. Stands watching his weeping grandchildren and the Khans as they fuss over the body in hammock. Then he takes several steps backward as the music and weeping grow louder and darkness eventually envelops the stage.

Lights Fade to Black.

Scene 3

Mid-morning. A few days later. It is the funeral of BAP. There will be a cremation at the foreshore. Sounds of gentle waves lapping against a beach. There is only a high pyre of about 4 feet high. There are several few mourners milling around. These include a number of Afro-Guyanese and people of non-Indian heritage. Kish is talking with a group of young people from the mixed race set. There are two Dougla girls in the group. Kish, whose head is shaved except for a single lock in the middle, and Gita are dressed in dhoti and Sari respectively as are Panditji, Rajiv and his wife, Padma. Ayube, Shaira and Yusuf are also present. Shaira is also dressed in a sari. Gita is in deep conversation with Rajiv the Pandit's son somewhere upstage right. Shaira catches sight of them.

Shaira: *To Yusuf*) Look! *Sura and Dura*[30]!

Yusuf: *Looks*) I don't see nothing!

Shaira: Look where Ayube looking!

Yusuf: *Looks and Sighs.*)

Shaira: They have no shame! Rajiv wife is not two weeks in the grave and Bap just pass away!

Yusuf: Shaira ....

Shaira: Huh! And they talking about respectability !(*She scans the crowd catches sight of Panditji and his wife. She grabs hold of Yusuf and makes her way towards them.*

Ayube: *Remains staring at Gita and Rajiv.*)

Shaira: Panditji!

Panditji: Yusuf. Shaira.

Shaira: I was wondering if me and Yusuf could talk to you a little bit...

Panditji: *Hesitates*) I have a *work*[31] today I

Shaira: Is about Gita....

Panditji: What about Gitangili....

92

Shaira: We will treat she good. Now that Bap gone, Kishna can't take care of she. Panditji. You could talk to she make she see reason...

Panditji: Shaira. I know you mean well. But you are Muslim!

Yusuf: These are modern times, man!

Panditji: Gitangili is a Hindu girl ! We have to find a Hindu match for her!

Shaira: You mean like you own son?!

Panditji: My son is mourning a dead wife!

Shaira: *Turns away*) It don't look so to me! (*Walks off in a huff.*)

Panditji: *Looks across at Gita and Rajiv. Beckons to Kish*) Kishna Beta....

Kishna: Yes...Panditji ?

Panditji: We are almost ready . Go get your sister.

Kishna: Uncertainly) Oh...ok.....

Panditji: You alright?

Kishna: I'm not sure....

Panditji: Like I told you....you don't have to worry, just follow my lead. Repeat everything that I say....

Kishna: Repeat everything you say...ok.

Panditji: And mimic every action you see me do.

Kish: Copy actions also.

Panditji: Remember it is very important to do everything precise if we are to set Bap's soul on its proper journey.

Kish: Is ok. Panditji....I understand. I will follow you without a mistake!

Panditji: *Looking across at where Gita is still in deep conversation with Rajiv*) I think we should get people together now.

Kish: *Follows his gaze and crosses to Rajiv and Gita. Crosses to Gita.*

93

Kishna: Gita! Rajiv!

Rajiv :You ready to start?

Kish: Ready as I will ever be....

Rajiv: Don't worry my father is the best Pandit around. You are in good hands! (*To Gita*.) Once again I am sorry for your loss.

Gita: And we're sorry for yours.

Rajiv: *Nods and goes to stand beside his mother.)*

Kish: Gita! That didn't look good! You shouldn't be alone talking with boys!

Gita: What?!

Kish: The whole mandir was watching you too, including Panditji!

Gita: Since when you care about anything like this?

Kish: Look go and take your place. We about to begin.

Gita: *Goes and stands in the front row of those now formed in a ragged circle around the pyre.)*

Panditji: Beloved brothers and sisters gather round! As you know we are here today to give the last rites to our father, brother and friend Bamsingh. In a few minutes I will light the *bedi*[32] and the religious ceremony will begin. So those of you who would like to view the earthly remains of our beloved Bamsingh please do so now.

A few people including Shaira but not Yusuf go forward. Panditji motions to Kish who comes to stand beside him.

Panditji: *To Kish*) Remember follow me.

Kish: *Swallows deeply and nods.)*

Panditji: *Begins to chant a prayer*) Om Shanti...Shanti....

Kish: *Closes his eyes. Adopts the Pandits exact physical stance. Starts to repeat after the Pandit but after two of three tries is unable to keep up. So he contents himself by closing his eyes tightly and moving his lips as though he is deep in prayer.*

94

After a while Panditji opens his own eyes and stops chanting as he is ready to light the pyre. But Kish whose eyes are still closed does not see this and a few long seconds pass uncomfortably before he realizes that he has to stop.

Panditji: *Coughs under his breath.)*

Kish: *Coughs also.)*

Panditji: *Touches Kish gently on his forearm.)*

Kish: *Without opening his eyes does the same.)*

People attending the cremation begin to notice something wrong and begin to whisper.

Shaira: Hindu nuh! Hindu my eye!

Yusuf. God Shaira. Is a funeral! People does get confused.!

Shaira: huh!

Panditji: Kishna! Open your eyes! It is time to light the pyre!

Kishna: *Repeating with the exact intonation)* Kishna! Open your eyes! It is time to light the pyre!

Panditji: *Ignores him and lights the pyre.)*

Kishna: *Startled by the sudden fire opens his eyes.)*

Pandit: Now pay attention! I'm going to chant five mantras. Don't bother to try to do the same. You walk around the fire five times and every time you hear me say "shanti" that means peace, I will hand you something to throw in and you must throw it in the flame.

Kish: More nervous than ever now, grabs Gita's hand and begins to walk)

Panditji: (Exasperated) Kishna! You have to do it alone!

Gita: Falls back and Kish walks around the pyre as the Pandit chants the mantras and hands him incense from his lotar wrapped around with Hibiscus flowers to throw into the pyre on each "shanti" As the fifth mantra is finished and Panditji says the last "shanti" the spirit of BAP rises from the pyre and stands behind Gita. No one else sees this.

95

Panditji: May he travel in peace. Om Shanti. Shanti. (*Motions to Rajiv and his wife*) Come let's go quick before something more embarrassing happen again!

Rajiv: I thought it went ok.....

Panditji: What you know eh? If wasn't for me you would be in the same boat as Kishna and Gitangili! Ignorant about your culture and religion!

Rajiv: But Bap....

Panditji: Don't talk back to me boy! Go bring the car and lets go!

Rajiv: But Bap....we promised to bring them home.....

Panditji: Only this one time and because their grandfather was a devoted Hindu. But not after today you hear me?! You don't have nothing in common with them! Plus you are a mourning widower. So act like one! (*Storms off with his wife following him.*) Damn *chamars*!

Rajiv: *Beckons to Gita and Kish.*

Lights Fade to Black.

Scene 4

A month later. Gita is swinging in the hammock on her veranda. She is singing along to a filmi song on the radio. Rajiv passes in front of their house on his way home. He waves as he passes and Gita calls out to him.

Gita: What happen like since Bap dead we turn strangers?!!

Rajiv: No! I just ...busy...you know....

Gita: *Coming to the front gate*) No. I don't know. Why don't you come tell me?

Rajiv: *Looking around*) Look Gitangili. You know how people like to take one thing and make it another. Better if people don't see us talking, right now.

Enter Shaira and Ayube into the front yard of their house.

Ayube: Waves.)

Shaira: Aye Gita! You entertaining?! (*Laughs*) How you do eh Rajiv?

96

Rajiv: Fine thanks Miss. Khan (*To Gita*) You see!

Gita: Don't worry with that woman. She can't do you nothing! Come and *gaff*[33] with me nuh? Kishna hardly home these days and Bap never let me get any friends, except you and the girls in the mandir[34].

Rajiv: No Gita! I have to go. Panditji will drive by here just now and.... (*Stops self-consciously.*)

Gita: And what?

Rajiv: Nothing. I got to go that's all! (*Begins to hurry off.*)

Gita: Rajiv! If something wrong tell me, but don't treat me so!

Rajiv: Gitangili. Sorry. I don't mean to hurt your feelings or anything. I just don't have a choice right now.

Gita: *Turns to go inside*) Ok. I won't bother you again.

Rajiv: *Turns to follow her and then stops himself*) Gitangili! Gitangili is not you...not me....I mean.../ 'ent have nothing against you-all!

Gita: *Sits in the hammock and begins to rock silently.*)

Rajiv: *Comes to sit quietly at the bottom of the stairs*) Gitangili....

Gita: *Sighs*) This must be how poor Ayube does feel....

Rajiv: Don't talk stupidness! You and Ayube different! Totally!

Gita: Is true. Everybody does treat he like ...like he got some terrible sick! You making me feel just so !

Rajiv: Gitanjili! No! Is not you....Look. I just trying to do the right thing.

Gita: Gitangili! You and Panditji are the only people who call me by my full name !

Rajiv: It is a wonderful name. You can almost her music when you say it...Gitangili.....

Gita: So why you don't want to talk to me?

Rajiv: I do everything Panditji tell me all my life. Is so they raise me to be. Baba and my mother.(*Sighs*) And for this thing to happen to me...this terrible thing to

97

happen to Savi and the baby!

Gita: I know. It sad your wife and baby died, but was not your fault, Raj.

Rajiv: So you think....

Gita: Why you say that?

Rajiv: *Is silent.*)

Gita: Raj...is that what's on your mind?

Rajiv: She was a beautiful, virtuous and wonderful girl.....

Gita: I know.

Rajiv: The best Panditji said....

Gita: Aha.

Rajiv: But I didn't love her!!!

Gita: What?!!!

Rajiv: I tried Gitangili. But I didn't couldn't. Now I am so sorry....

Gita: But maybe in time. You all was only married for ten months. Bap used to say love is a long, twist-up dam-top[35]!

Rajiv: Duty matters more than love, my Panditji says.

Gita: I believe in love still...

Rajiv: Love is the rule of the passions. A true Brahman is not subject to passion....(*Laughs.*)

Gita: Bap used to say somethings like that too.

Rajiv: She knew, you know.

Gita: Knew what?

Rajiv: I didn't love her.

Gita: How?!

Rajiv: She asked me.

Gita: And you told her?!!

Rajiv: I didn't answer. But that in itself was an answer. She died having my child and knowing that she was not loved!! (*Sobs.*)

Gita: Ohh! Raj. Sorry. I sorry bad!

Rajiv: That's why she is haunting me now!!!

Gita: What?!!

Rajiv: Every night. I see her. She comes and lies down next to me and she tells me, " I will always love you Rajiv!"

Gita: An what you do?!!

Rajiv: I wake up and don't go back to sleep again.

Gita: *Every* night?!

Rajiv: *Nods.*)

Gita: Gosh! Does your father know?

Rajiv: No!

Gita: But you should tell him! He is a Pandit. He will know what to do!

Rajiv: Panditji can't fix every problem in the world.

Gita: But this is a spiritual one! Who better than he to help? I remember when I was a small girl. I used to see my father all the time with the cutlass coming, coming. Bap took me by a Mandir and after the Pandit look after me. I never see that spirit again.

Rajiv: So you think Panditji can help make Savitri go away?

Gita: Yes. He got powers. People say he is the best Pandit around.

Rajiv: Uhmmmmm. (*Pauses*) Gitangili...you ever dream Bap?

Gita: Yes. He dream me two time since he dead. But he just watching. He don't tell me nothing. Is not like he trying to frighten me or anything. You know, just like he there watching, like that.

99

Rajiv: He was an alright old man.

Gita: He liked you a whole lot Rajiv...

Rajiv: He alone?

Gita: Rajiv!!!

Rajiv: Come on ....answer.....

Gita: I....

Enter Panditji suddenly. He storms over from his house in anger.)

Panditji: Rajiv!

Rajiv: *Gets up hurriedly and goes to meet his father*) Baba!

Gita: Good night Panditgi!

Pandit: *To Gita*) Young girl go inside (*To Rajiv*)You are determined to bring disgrace down on me nuh?

Rajiv: What did I do?

Panditji: You and Gitangili! Right there in front of the whole world and for the terrible neighbors to see!!!

Rajiv: Panditji we were just talking.

Panditji: Everything starts off with talking boy! She is a young girl seventeen and you are a young man twenty-two. You were alone without supervision! Disgraceful!

Rajiv: Baba, these are modern times. Plus we were in full view of the public....

Panditji: *Reaching their house*) You are looking for trouble boy! And you looking to bring shame on the good name of your family! What you think Savitri family going to say when they hear about this?! That you kill their daughter because you wanted another girl?!

Rajiv: What?!

Pandit: People will talk. They will say anything that seems reasonable!

100

Rajiv: How many times have I got to tell you that I don't care what people say?!

Panditji: Well you ought to care! Because your reputation is worth more than money in this country!

Rajiv: Sorry Panditji. I am sorry (*Enters the house.*)

Pandit: I am an old man. I know things that you don't know (*Turns to enter his house.*) You think I will let my only child fall prey to the ways of this world? You were born this time for great things....

Rajiv: Great things Baba? Great things? Then why am I so unhappy?!

Panditji: It is proper. You are mourning!

Rajiv: Is it proper too from my dead wife to haunt me? Every night? Night after night?!

Panditji: What?!

Rajiv: Yes!

Panditji: Impossible!

Rajiv: She has become a Churile! You didn't do the rites properly!

Panditji; How dare you? How dare you blame me for afflictions you create in your own life?!

Rajiv: Your hand is upon everything in my life, Baba. Everything. (*Exits.*)

Pandit: Calling after him) Raj! Rajiv! It is our culture! My father's hand is upon me too! You hear me? And his father upon him and his father's father! It is who we are boy!

Enter Padma. *She places some tea on the table.*

Panditji: You hear? You heard what your son said to me?!

Padma: *Nods and lays a gentle hand upon Pandiji's arm.)***She Exits.**

Enter Kishna. *He is about to pass Panditji's house and hails out to Panditji.*

Kishna: Night Panditji!

Panditji: *Does not answer but closes his front door firmly and nosily.)*

Dead Black Out.

Scene 5

Later that same night on the Bamsingh's veranda. Gita is lying in the hammock in tears.

Kish: Geet! What happen?

Gita: Nothing.

Kish: Come on tell me, please?

Enter Auybe. *He stands close to the fence and points in the direction of Panditji's house.)*

Kish: Panditji....

Ayube: *Shakes his head and mimics how Rajiv walks.)*

Kish: Rajiv!

Ayube: *Nods.)*

Kishna: *Pauses uncertainly, then)* Gita? Rajiv....he... did something to you?

Gita: *Continues to weep.)*

Kish: Gita. I can't read tear stains. You have to talk to me. Is this something to do with Panditji?

Gita: *Nods.)*

Kish: I knew it! Tonight I passed his house and he refused to say goodnight!

Gita: He hates us!

Kish: Why?!

Gita: We have no class. We'e not on his level!

Kish: That can't be true. He was always nice to us ....

Gita: Is since the funeral. The girls at the Mandir say is because *you* didn't do the rituals properly!

Kish: But he knows that I didn't know what to do?

Gita: That's why!!! Now he thinks I ignorant about religious things just like you!! He think I not good enough too!

Kish: Good enough for what?!

Gita: *Sobs.)*

Kish: Gitangili.....

Gita: *Sobs.)*

Kish: *Sighs)* Look. You can't let other people upset you so! Religion is good, but in the end is who you are inside that make you good enough. Not what other people think! And Geet...you good...you good-good-good!

Gita. I love him Kish!

Kish: Gita you are only 17 years....

Gita: I know how I feel!

Kish: Give it some time. You might see somebody nicer you know....

Gita: Bap wanted me to marry Rajiv and you have to carry out his wishes!

Kish: He didn't give me that particular instruction Gita!

Gita: Kish! You got to do something! You got to help me!

Kish: Look Gita. I don't know the first thing about matching ok. You and Rajiv got to fix that for yourselves.

Gita: You know that's not the way we do things.

Kish: Well what you want *me* to do eh Gita?!! I telling you I don't know what to do and I don't know!!!

Gita: You shoulda pay attention to Bap when he was trying to school you! But not you ! You was too busy with your Dougla girl!

Kish: What?!

Gita: Delicia! You think people don't know!

Kish: How *you* know about Delicia?!

Gita: She used to call for you....

Kish: And how come you never give me any message?

Gita: Bap tell me not to.

Kish: And you listened to him?

Gita: I didn't want you to get in trouble, Kish! Bap knew she was Black!

Kish: Her mother is Indian.

Gita: Bap say she Black.

Kish: How he know that?

Gita: Mr. Abrams up the road said he see you with a wavy hair girl by the UG[36] car park plenty times. Bap put two and two together. He said no Hindu girl won't name Delicia and he ask her straight one time she call.

Kish: *Laughs bitterly*) That explains it! **Exits inside the house.**

Gita: *Follows him*) Kish....don't vex with me. Bap make me do it!

Kish: That girl was my best friend at university. My study mate. You and Bap make her stop talk to me.

Gita: She Black Kish!

Kish: She is a human being Gita!

Gita: But she was a distraction Bap said! You have to study!
Kish: I see her everyday and she won't talk to me. Because of you and Bap! *That* is a distraction!

Exits to the bedroom.

Gita: *Does not follow, but goes into the kitchen and brings his food. She places it*

104

on the table along with a single letter.)

Enter Shaira and Yusuf. They knock on the front door.

Kish: I will get it! (*Comes out shirtless and opens the door.)*

Yusuf: Night Kish.

Kish: Night Mr. Khan.

Shaira: We can come in ?

Kish: Ah...yes...yes.....

Shaira: Sorry to come so late but that's the only time we can catch you home.

Kish: I working and studying now that Bap gone.

Yusuf: Must be hard for you alone eh?

Kish: I will make it.

Shaira: We would like to help....

Yusuf: You and Gita come like our own children....

Shaira: Yes! I couldn't help seeing the landlady come by again today for the rent and Gita lock up like nobody was home. I coulda tell she Gita was here but I say that is none of she damn business!

Yusuf: I could so with some help down at the shop, you know a cashier.

Kish: Look my hands full right now....

Shaira: No! Not you! We know you busy! Gitangili. We offering she the job.

Kish: I don't know....Gita is young. Bap never meant for her to work....

Shaira: She wouldn't have to if you would accept the marriage offer....

Kish: You know something. I don't own Gita! I can't make her decisions for her. You ask her yourself ok? You put the proposal to her and get it over once and for all!!! (*Calls*) Gitangili!

Shaira and Yusuf exchange uncomfortable glances.)

105

Kish: Gita! I said to come out here!

Yusuf: Look. It don't call for this man....

Kish: Gita!!! (*Goes into the kitchen and drags her out.*) You have a decision to make ok? When you decide let me know ! (*To Yusuf and Shaira*) Goodnight (*Picks up the tray and letter and goes into his bedroom.*)

Gita: Kish! Whatever you want me to do, I will do! Just tell me !

Kish: *Turning back*) You see ? This is the thing! You want *me* tell *you* what to do?!! You think I know? You think I myself know what to do? Girl! I want you to learn to make your own decision! Make up your own mind! Start learning to look after yourself little bit 'because running your life and my own is too much for me ok? Too much !

Shaira: Ow....boy it hard for you alone. We know....

Kish: *Shoots them a glance.*)

Gita: *Softly*) Kish...you know my heart.

Kish: laughs bitterly over his shoulder) *Your* heart Gita? *Your* heart?

Shaira: You can't think 'bout heart in these times. You got to think about food on the table and security...

Kish: Thinking like that 'cause my father to kill my mother....I can't choose that for my sister. If she want it for herself, I will stand by her. But I won't choose it.

Gita: Thank you for the offer Uncle Yusuf and Aunt Shaira. But I can't marry Ayube.

Yusuf: But take the job Beti. You will be safe with we at the store....

Gita: I take your job I will feel beholden to you....

Yusuf: No! You can get the job without any strings attached Beti!

Gita: Kish and me going to have to discuss it.

Yusuf: What kind of people you think we is eh, that you won't even accept we help, eh? What you think we will do to you-all?

Kish: Uncle...is not you. Is not nothing to do with who you are. ...

106

Shaira: *Rises and makes for the door*) Well Miss Gita. If you think Pandit son going to *knot he dhoti with you sari*[37], you better think again!

Yusuf: *Follows her*) Think about the job Gita...

Shaira: *Pulling a letter from her bosom*) OH! The land lady leave this for you all today

Kish: *Takes it and tears the letter open.*)

Shaira: If you all can't find a place to move, you always welcome to come stay with me. I have a lot a space !

She and Yusuf Exit.

Kish: *Sinks to a chair*) Ow Bap! Why you gone and leave we in this eh? Why?!

Gita: *Hugs her brother*) I'm sorry Kish. We going to think of something Kish. I will find a job and help out! We will think of something!

Kish: Bap ....Bap ow Bap........(*Weeps.*)

Enter Bap in spirit. *He is dressed in white Dhoti. As he enters he knocks over the Bhagvadgita on the shelf in the sitting room. Gita and Kish glances.*

Kish: *Picks up the book and looks at the page that is open. He smiles.*)

Bap settles into a corner and smiles.

The lights fade to Black.

Scene 6
Three weeks later. At Panditji's house. Kishna knocks on the door and Rajiv answers.

Rajiv: Kish! What's up?

Kish: Is your father home yet?

Rajiv: Yes. He is praying. You will have to wait a while...

Kish: Oh......

Rajiv: What ? Are you in a hurry?

Kish: It's Gita. The Sukanti is attacking her again!

Rajiv: What? But I thought Panditji fixed that last week?

Kish: I don't know. But she is in a really bad way. You should see her, like skin and bone. The thing like it sucking the life our of her, day by day.

Rajiv: Hmmmmmm. He didn't help me, and he didn't help Gitangili......

Enter Panditji.

Panditji: Who didn't help who?

Rajiv: *Does not answer but turns away*) Kish is here to see you....

Panditji: Is Raj ok?

Kish: I don't know....

Panditji: Did you tell him something to upset him? What are you doing here anyway?!

Kish: I really hate to bother you again. But you are the only one who can help. Gitangili...the Sukanti....

Panditji: She still suffering?!! Impossible?!!

Kish: She is thin as a razor grass. I took her to the doctor today. He say's he can't find any reason why she is just wasting away like that. Everybody say you're the *onliest*[38] man who can help.

Panditji: Really? People know that she still being attacked?!

Kish: Yes...I am afraid so....

Panditji: Look! I can't be associated with this...this....case. It is not good for my reputation!

Enter Rajiv dressed for the road.

Rajiv: I am going to go and see her !

Panditji: Why?! What can you do? You not sorry for yourself boy!?

Rajiv: She suffers like I suffer. I feel for her!

Panditji: Rajiv! I forbid you to leave this house!

Rajiv: I forbid you to run my life!

Panditji: Slaps him hard.)

Rajiv rubs his face, stares at his father and then Exits.

Panditji: To Kish) This is all your fault! Turning my son against me! You and your sister! Dragging him into adharma[39]!

Kish: Sorry Panditji.. I am going to look for another Pandit to try to save my sister.

Panditji: Why can't you just accept that it is her destiny to go this way and let the divine order take it's natural course?

Kish: Destiny? It is Gita's destiny to die of this ghostly affliction? And what about Rajiv? Is he too to suffer the visitations of the Churilie for the rest of his life? Your own son?!

Panditji: He has his karma to work out! I can't interfere!

Kish: Shakes his head and turns to go) Sorry to bother you. I will find someone else. **Exits.**

Panditji: Shouts after him.) There is no other! I am the Panditji!!

Kish: Crosses to his house.)

Gita: Is lying in the hammock feigning illness.)

Kish: You can relax. Is just me alone. He's not coming.

Gita: What?!

Kish: Right. So we back to square one.

Gita: You got to think of something else Kish! Rajiv was just here, holding my hand and confessing how much he cares for me!

Kish: So where is he now?

Gita: He went to Ms. Abrams shop to get some chicken noodle soup.

109

Kish: You good, you know! Chicken noodle soup?!!!

Gita: *Laughs.*)

Kish: It's just as well anyway. That boy has his own problems and I didn't feel comfortable with this thing at all.

Enter Panditji.

Kish: *Gasping*) Pa...Panditji!

Panditji: For the sake of your Bap. I going to try one more time.

Gita: *Sinks into the hammock and lets out a loud groan.*)

Panditji: *To Kish*) She can sit up straight?

Kish: I don't know (*Tries to get her up but she flops back down again.*)

Panditji: Ok. Just get a sheet from inside. We will have to lie her down flat on the floor.

Kish Exits to the bedroom.

Panditji busies himself with his books and incense.)

Gita sneaks a good look at him every time she thinks he is not watching.)

Enter Rajiv. He pauses upon seeing his father.

Panditji: Come...come Raj....

Enter Kish.
Kish spreads the sheet. Lifts his almost lifeless sister and puts her on the sheet. Then he begins to shudder.)

Panditji: Kish?! Boy you ok?!

Kish: What?

Rajiv: You sure you ok?!

Kish: Of course !

Panditji: Now you will have to do what I tell you..

110

Kish begins to shudder again and this time grabs Gita and begins to speak in Hindi.)

Panditji: What?! Kishna?

Rajiv: Oh! My God!

Kish continues and as he does so Gitangili comes back to full health, sits up, smiles at everyone and then rises and stretches.)

Panditji: Gitangili? Is that you?

Gita: *Giggling cheerfully)* Who else could it be?! Can I get you something to drink?

Kish is now back to himself and sits down in a daze.)

Rajiv: Baba! Did you see that? Did you?

Panditji: Yes...I did....

Rajiv: He cured her Bap! Kishna saved her life! *(To Kish)* How did you do it man? You always said you don't believe in these things?!

Panditji: *Packing up his bag)* It was not Kishna doing anything, Raj, Lord Shiva was here.

Kishna: I saw it as clear as the Bel Air sky Panditji! Rajiv and Gita and the great lord driving them in a chariot!

Panditji: What?!!

Rajiv: Really?

Panditji: In a chariot? You sure about that?

Kish: Yes. Sure.

Panditji: *Picking up his bags)* I see....

Kish: Well you not going to marry them?!

Panditji: I have to consult my books Kishna, and then I will get the full story.

Gita: Full story?

111

Panditji: Yes...of what really happened here today. I am a deeply religious man. My ways may be ancient. But they are sure. (*To Rajiv*) You bought soup eh? **Exits.**

Rajiv: *Looking confused*) I don't get it?! He should be happy...she is cured ! Instead he seems so angry and kind of sad!

Gita and Kish exchange knowing glances.)

Rajiv: Maybe you can help me too then? Help me nah Kish?!

Kish: Ah...you ....heard what you father said. It was Shiva ! Not me!

Rajiv: But try! Try ! Please!

Kish puts his hands on Rajiv's shoulders and then his head and tries but nothing happens) Sorry Raj. Maybe we can try again sometime...maybe your father will help you now.

Rajiv: But why?! Why Shiva came for Gitanjili and not for me?! Why?!

Kish: Raj. Look. Don't give up hope man. Don't take it so hard....

Rajiv: Six months now! Every night I can't sleep...this ...pregnant spirit haunting me! Sometimes I feel like I could drink some Gramazone or something! Kish. You all don't know!

Kish: No! Don't commit suicide! No! (*Looks at Gita. Takes a deep breath*) Raj. I know. I know how awful things playing in your head over and over could be...You need to get medical help.

Rajiv: No medical doctor can't help me!

Kish: Maybe. Maybe it might be something else bothering you and not the Churile. You know making you think about death and killing yourself....

Rajiv: You trying to say I *mental* or something?!

Kish: Raj....

Gita: Kish!

Raj: I did say your sister was running off?! Like I have nowhere to turn! How you could say something like that to me?! I have nobody to turn to (*Rises.*)

Kish: *Grabs him by the shoulders)* Raj! You have people! God didn't desert you! Don't say that! Look what happened here tonight....

Gita: *Grabs him)* Kish! No!

Kish: He is suffering Gita! We have to tell him!

Rajiv: What are you talking about? What is going on!

Gita: No! No! It will ruin everything!

Kish: *Shaking off her arm)* If he is your heart Gita, then you should feel it breaking.

Rajiv: What is it? Tell me?

Gita: *Sobs)* No...no...

Kish: You want him to kill himself?

Gita: *Shakes her head.)* No!

Kish: *Takes a deep breath)* Rajiv...your burden's are too great . We can't add to them. Gita was not sick. Ah...that... it was a trick.

Rajiv: What...I ...don't...a trick?!

Gita: *Nods and sinks to the floor in sobs.)*

Rajiv: Why?!

Kish: *Goes to sit in a chair. His head in his hands.)* Sorry man. Sorry...

Rajiv: *Angry)* Why?!

Kish: Ayyyyyy! What can I say? So much...so much of our lives *full-up* with corners we can't turn, lights at the end of deep *Kokers* swimming outside our hand-reach! Endless frustration... Things that we want...tantalize us and the walls that people build cramp us in...ahhh..choke us in! No ! Because I said so! No because you can't! No because that's just the way it is! Too many no's and too few how to's....Till a darkening hoplessness descends and covers your eyes, speaks in your ears, walks in your dreams, steals your spirit like a Sukanti! And the one thing that's left is the bottle...Gramazone in one hand....alcohol in the next...either way...

Rajiv: *Advancing)* You tricked me! *And* my father! My *entire* family! And this is

113

your reason? That you were frustrated because someone told you NO?!!

Kish: No! I mean....

Rajiv: It is our culture Kish. I am proud of who we are!

Gita: We are too!

Rajiv: Then why?

Ayube emerging from under the veranda.

Ayube: Because Gita cry for you!

Rajiv: Gitanjili?!

Kish: Yes! For my sister ! And the crazy idea of hers that she loves *you*!

Rajiv: Me?!

Kish: Sorry man....

Rajiv: *Goes to sit in the hammock and begins to rock back and forth slowly. He reaches over and pets Gitangli's head and begins to hum a filimi song with the words Gitanliji.)*

Kish: Raj...you ok man?

Rajiv : *Sighs)* Ahhhhhhhh! I don't know what the future holds Kishna. But at this moment . I am free!

Gita rests her head against Rajiv's leg as Ayube rocks the hammock gently.)

Kish: *Regards them for a moment. Rises)* Ah...I'll be back in a short while...there is ...ah....there is someone I really need to see.... **Exits .**

Light slowly fade to Black on Mohamed Raffi's Soundtrack, "*The World is One.*"

The End.

Glossary and Notes for Sukanti

[1] *Jhandi* - Commonly refers to the colored flags attached to bamboo poles used by Hindu's to mark religious work. However, the original word *Jhandi* itself, referred to the type of religious rite marked by flags and not the flags alone.

[2] *Pandit* - Hindu Priest. "Gi" - suffix used to refer to a person held in very high esteem, almost sainthood.

[3] *Abe or a (h)we* - our.

[4] *Tek am in* - take it in. Absorb it.

[5] *Preposition* - Proposal

[6] *Beti* - granddaughter. Also may be used for daughter or niece.

[7] *Rass* - your ass or rump. Expression peculiar to the West Indies. May have several other meanings as well depending on the context. For instance "Oh rass!" can be an expression of great admiration or of great trepidation.

[8] *Jabberjasty* - Hotheaded /rash.

[9] *Ya* - Here.

[10] *Phagala / Phaggaly* - Deformed person, mongoloid or mentally handicapped.

[11] *Chapat* - person of lower caste. Used as a derogatory term.

[12] *Karma* - Law of Kharma dictates that a person will be reborn in a subsequent life according to his morality and the way he lives his subsequent or present life. As such *bad karma* is now sometimes taken to mean literally negative vibrations which can affect ones present and future lives adversely.

[13] *That ent concern ayo* - It does not concern you.

[14] *Arredy* – Already.

[15] *Wha da fuh ?* - What is that for?/ Why?

[16] *Gi* - Give

[17] *Bhai* - Boy

[18] *Nah mek* - Don't allow. Don't cause.

[19] *Sukanti* - Evil Indian spirit that possess children and young girls eventually killing them. Sometimes associated with jealousy of female spirit or with the lust of a male spirit. It is said that they can attach themselves through hair left flowing during the night.

[20] *Renk* - Rank or impurities. Usually associated in Hindu religious terms with the consumption of meat and fish.

[21] *Aloo Parata and Hassar Curry*- Potato roti/ unleavened bread with a curry of a particular sweet water fish known also as *Cascadoo*. It has a bony dark exoskeleton and is found in swamps associated with cane fields and rice fields also.

[22] *Nara* - Intense belly ache associated with twisted intestines. Many older East Indian's attribute any illness to this condition which they say can be easily cured by a gifted *'nointer* or masseuse.

[23] *Nah* - Cannot. No. Will not, depending on the context. In this case it means will not.

[24] *Yag* - Religious meeting which lasts for several days.

[25] *Mush-hi-ke-re* - Certain type of bird associated with bad omens and death. Family of the Jumbie bird or bird of the sprits.

[26] *Get you Docta paper* - Become certified as a doctor. Get the certificate.

[27] *Chamar* - Very low caste person.

[28] *Bhagvadgita* – A Hindu scriptural book.

[29] *Beta* - My son

[30] *Suru and Duru* - Fabled inseparable lovers of Caribbean East Indian mythology.

[31] *Work* - Commonly used to refer to the performance of Hindu or Muslim religious ceremony.

[32] *Bedi* - Pyre

[33] *Gaff-* Talk a while

[34] *Mandir* - Hindu place of worship.

[35] *Dam* - top : High dirt road usually on the bank of a river or deep trench.

[36] *UG* - University of Guyana

[37] *Knot he dhoti with you sari* - Marry you. Making the allusion to part of the Hindu marriage ritual where the brides sari and grooms dhoti of cloth from them both is tied together.

[38] *Onliest* – Peculiar old Indo- Guyanese usage for "only". Reads as "only-only".

[39] *Adharma* – (Sanskrit) Spritually evil forces as defined in the Gita's.

Churile – Spirit of a woman who has died in childbirth. Seen on streets at night. Haunts and can kill women in childbirth and their babies.

Anansi's Way
A Play in One Act
by Paloma Mohamed
Winner of the Guyana Prize for Literature

Anansi (Anancy) – African Spider God who "harbors knowledge in folk tales and weaves words."
Maureen Warner Lewis – Guineas Other Suns.

Estimated running time : 70 to 90 minutes.

List of Characters:

1. Nancy : Male student form 4C. Skinny and studious. Good looking but wears glasses.
2. Vanessa: Female student. Form 4C. Very attractive.
3. Baba : Janitor. In his seventies.
4. Leon : Portuguese male student from C. Handsome and very flashy. Likes to be called LION.
5. Samantha: Black female student of form 4C. Very pretty. Leon's girlfriend.
6. Jassnarine/Jass: Indian male student in form 4C.
7. Susie: Female student in form 4C. Jass's girlfriend.
8. Keith: Male student in form 4C.
9. Mahidai/Tracy : Indian female student in form 4C and Keith's girlfriend.
10. Miss Richards: Form teacher of form 4C and literature teacher.
11. Boy 1: Hector - in lower form than fourth.
12. Boy 2: Jerry -in lower form than fourth.
13. Boy 3: Ossie -in lower form than fourth.
14. Extras: This play can include as many extras as possible for crowd scenes.

The Action: The play is set in a classroom and front yard of Milton's Way High School.
The entire action takes place over two weeks.

The Set: This play is set in a modern classroom. There are single chairs and desks at which students will sit singly. This arrangement also allows for easy manipulation of the furniture as will become necessary in some scenes. There are about 12 chairs and desks. A chalkboard is mounted upon a wall at stage left. A big red fluffy cloth duster hangs on the wall upstage and next to the chalkboard. There is a simple wooden table and chair in front of the class, which serves as a teacher's desk. Part of the schoolyard is visible. Here the dominant article is large mange tree halfway up whose bark a basketball hoop is nailed.

119

Scene 1

Monday morning around 8.55 am. Spotlight up upon a hand cleaning the board with the big red duster. Only the hands and arms are visible.

Baba: *a loud sputtering cough escapes*) How I going to begin to tell this story? (*Coughs again*)
Such things does happen in life, good things and nobody don't write about them! Ayyyyy! No TV don't have them on the news and none of them dub poets don't sing about them. But this story...this particular story! This one going to be known..(*Finishes cleaning the board.*) This story is about a boy ...

Lights up on the schoolyard as Nancy shoots a basketball into the hoop.

Baba: *Continues*) and a girl .

Enter Vanessa.

Baba: Lovely child!

Vanessa walks directly past Nancy and into the class room. As Vanessa passes all the boys in the school yard turn to look. Some catcall.

The lights fade up in the classroom.

Baba exits to the school yard. *Begins to sweep.*

Baba: *Sweeping*) Is a story about another set of boys and girls too!

Enter Leon on the motorbike with Samantha as the pillion rider. Then Jass and Keith enter carrying Susie and Tracy on their bikes .

Baba swishes his broom in the direction of the gate just as the motor bike and bicyclers all speed into the yard. They stir up a lot of dust which almost covers Baba.

Baba bursts into another fit of coughing.

Leon dismounts his bike laughing raucously. Jass, Keith, Susie and Tracy join in.

120

Baba: *Sighs loudly*) Ahhhhhhhhhhhy! (*Pulls a large rag out of his pocket and puts it over his face like a mask and continues to sweep*) Moon ah run till day ketch am![1]

The newcomers sit around on their bikes laughing and chatting. The school bell rings once. They ignore it. It rings a second time. Nancy appears and takes his seat near the front of the class. Vanessa is already sitting in the second row. The bell rings a third time. The group in the yard still does not respond.

The bell rings again for the fourth time. *In the school yard the loitering continues. Baba walks over to the group.*

Baba: Fourth bell! You all can't be loitering out here!

Leon: Bell? You all hear any bell?!

The others laugh.

Leon: *to Baba*) You sure you hear right? You wearing your hearing aid today?

Baba: Look you young hooligan! I have perfectly good everything, which is much more than you could ever wish for when you get to my age! You all either go inside or go home. Take your pick! But you can't-stay- out-here-no-more! And dat is final!

Jass: *To others*) Come let we go in man....

Leon: What?!

Jass: I said ....

Leon: Don't repeat it man! (*To others*) You all believe this faggot? (*Mimics Jass*) "Come let we go in man..." (*Laughs.*)

Samantha: He spend too much time by he grandmother in the country! (*Walks over to Jass and pushes him in the chest*) You getting soft!

Jass: Ay girl! Watch it!

Leon: *You* watch how you talking to my woman, Jass! Don't make the mistake and 'diss[2] Samantha boy! 'Cause you done know !

Baba: Ok ! I closing the gate now! Who staying stay! And who going go! (*Advances to the gate.*)

Leon: *Kick starts his bike*) I outa here!

121

Samantha: Not without me! (*Jumps onto the back of the bike. Motions to Susie and Tracy*) You all try with them two losers!

Leon: *Motions to Susie*) I have room for one more Sue!

Susie looks at Jass, then back at Leon.

Jass: If you go with him! We done!

Susie: Look! Don't threaten me Jass! I wasn't planning to go!

Jass: Oh! Ho!

Leon: Birds of a feather flock together! Soft girl for soft boy!

Susie: *Advancing to Leon*) Well is who you really think you talking to ?!

Jass: *Holding her back*) Come let we go!

Leon: *to Keith and Tracy*) I guess the two of you all staying too?

Tracy: *Picking up Keith's bike and jumping on*) No way! Monday morning and boring Miss. Richards?! Keith if you staying...I going with Leon dem!

Keith: *Looks undecided*) Baba already close the gate...

Leon: *Laughs*) Not a problem (*Walks over to the gate and picks the lock.*) Freedom!

Jass: *To Susie)* Let's go!

Leon: You all go in there and forget about being friends with me!

Jass and Susie wave and go inside.

Leon: *Shouts after them*) Gwan[3], let dem teach you to be like a rotten banana! Gwan!

Lyon kicks his bike into action and exits. Tracy jumps on Keith's bike and tries to keep up with Lyon. When Keith realizes that he will be left behind he runs and jumps unto the carrier and they exit.

Enter Baba .

122

Baba: *Looks around)* These children believe they know everything! That the couple hours they have to spend in school they will miss out on so much life! (*Inspects the lock on the gate*) Yet…they really don't know nothing about life…(*Drops the lock back to the gate*) Huh! At least he didn't mash it up. (*Closes the gate and padlocks it again.*) **Exits.**

Lights up on the classroom. Susie and Jass enter.

Miss Richards: *Looking at her watch)* You all lucky. One minute more and I would have marked you absent!

Jass: Sorry…

Miss Richards: Take your seats.

Susie and Jass take seats next to each other at the back of the class.

Miss Richards: Where are the others?

Susie: We don't know!

Miss Richards: *We* don't know? What happen Jass hire a lawyer? You talking for him now?

Nancy and Vanessa start to giggle.

Jass: *Pelting a tap behind the head of Nancy)* Shut up four-eye!

Miss Richards: That's enough! I asked a question Jass and I want an answer.

Jass: How I will know where they are? I here and they not here! That is all I could say!

Miss Richards: I thought I saw you all outside when I was coming into the classroom this morning?

Susie: Look like dis is a police investigation or what? I thought this was a classroom!

Miss Richards: Point taken. So let's not waste any more time. You guys have to finish a good part of the syllabus still and with all these strikes and disturbances that have been taking place we are behind. (*She rises, take up the books on her desk and places one on each student's desk.*)

Susie: *Picks up the book and gives a long suck teeth)* Steeeeeeeeeeeeeeeeeeewps!

123

Jass: The legend of Anansi? This is what they have people learning for CXC! I shoulda really go with Leon dem this morning!

Miss Richards: *Gives him a hard look, but says nothing. She writes on the board " The Legends of Anansi.")* Now has anybody here heard of Anansi before?

All: Yes!

Miss Richards: Good! Then each of you can tell me what you heard! Vanessa?

Vanessa: Miss he was a spider!

Miss Richards: Good! Yes, he was a spider!

Susie: *Pointing to Nancy)* And he wore some big round glasses and was in form 4 C! (*Does a high five with Jass as they both laugh.*)

Miss Richards: Very funny Susie! I hope you will laugh like that when you see your grades!

Susie: Sorry! So Anansi was a spider and he was very evil or something like that! I don't really remember...

Miss Richards: He is sometimes thought of as wily..,

Susie: No! Evil was not really the word I was looking for... is more like "cockish[4]" you know...

Vanessa: Yes! A smart-man!

Susie: Who ask you anything pork face!

Miss Richards: Susie! Look ! It's too early in the morning for this! Stop being so unkind to people! You wouldn't want to be called names!

Susie: Nobody can't dis me like that! Cause they done know that I would beat them down and when I finish, Jass would whip them down and then...

Miss R: That's enough! (*Takes a deep breath*) Anansi, was not dishonest, not really. But why do you think that people sometimes give him this quality ?

Jass: (*Tossing down the book*)Why do *you* think we should study this stupidness for CXC?!

124

Miss Richards: Patience. You will see. Nancy, we haven't heard from you for this whole morning?

Susie: *Muttering under her breath)* Sissy!

Miss Richards: *Glares at her)* Nancy?

Nancy: What was the question?

Miss Richards: Anansi. Why do you know about him?

Nancy: Well he was an African God or something !

Miss Richards: Really? I didn't know that?

Nancy: Yes! Says it right here in the introduction to the book...

Miss Richards: Right yes! The spider god of the Ashanti peoples of Africa.

Vanessa: And he was the story teller or the keeper of the stories of the African people before writing was popular!

Miss Richards: Right! So, the word Anansi, or *nancy* itself means "story".

Jass: Really? So we have a long fine[5] *story* sitting up in front there (*Pointing to Nancy.)*

Miss Richards: So Susie, what kind of Anansi stories you heard when you were growing up?

Susie: I don't remember. My .....I don't remember!

Miss Richards: But you must remember something ...come on try...

Susie: No! I don't want to remember no nancy story!

Jass: Cool it!

Susie: *Storms out of the class leaving all her books.)*

Jass: *Grabs his and Susie's books and follows her)* Gotta go!

Miss Richards: *Calls after them)* Read chapter one for homework! (*Turns back to the rest of the class with a big smile*) Now.....where were we ?

The bell goes. Dead Black Out.

Scene 2

Immediately afterwards. Lights up on the schoolyard. Enter Susie in a big rush. She is heading for the gate. She is followed by Jass running. He reaches her just a few feet away from the gate.

Jass: Sue! Wait up! (*Grabs her arm.*)

Sue: *Trying to shrug him off*) Leave me alone!

Jass: I know you don't mean that! (Hands her the books) You left these....

Susie: *Looks at them, gives a long suck teeth and turns away*) Steweeeeeeeeeeps!

Jass: You know I really, really confused Sue? I don't get it? How you turn up like spoil milk so all of a sudden?

Susie: I shoulda never come here today!

Jass: Why?

Susie: None of your business!

Jass: *Holding her by the shoulders*) Aye! Look is *me* you talking to! Me Jass! You don't have no business that is not my business girl!

Susie: Is nothing ! Truly!

Jass: Something upset you in there and I want to know what! You know I could fix them....

Susie: You can't fix this Jass...

Jass: I could fix anything! Just tell me....

Susie: *Snapping*) I said you can't fix this! You can't ! Nobody can!

Jass: Look. Take your books....

Susie refuses to take them.

126

Jass: *Pushes the books at her)* Take them!

Susie: I didn't tell you to bring them! You shoulda left them on the desk!

Jass: Girl look! Whatever is bugging you I don't know. But you getting weird! You make me miss the end of the class for nothing!

Susie: That stupid Anansi class?! You should thank me! You didn't miss nothing!

Jass: We don't know! We were not there...

Susie: Why she had to make us talk about Anansi....

Jass: It on the syllabus....

Susie: Give me maths any day.

Jass: *Laughs)* You? Maths?!

Susie: At least everything is black and white. One and one make two. The answer either wrong or right! But that Ms. Richards, she like to make people think too much...too much about their own life...

Jass: A little thinking never kill nobody!

Susie: Speak for yourself!

Jass: Susie, you freaking out over nothing! These Anansi stories is not nothing so deep to think about.

Susie: So you think....

Jass: But I thought you say you couldn't remember anything about Anansi....

Susie: At first I couldn't.

Jass: And then what happen?

Susie: Jass. Drop it!

Jass: No...tell me...and then?

Susie: And then I began to remember. I began to remember a lot a things....my Grandmother and the stories...

Jass: So great! What wrong with that!

Susie: You would never understand ok!

Jass: I thought I was your heart and your soul girl? How you doing me like this? How you wouldn't talk to me?

Susie: *Laughs*) Your heart and soul? You don't even know me! (*Walks off.*)

Jass: *Stunned*) Huh?!

Enter Baba.

Baba: Boy! What you doing out here ? You know you can't be out here in the middle of the period!

Jass: I…Baba….Sorry… (*Turns to go inside.*)

Baba: She got a story to tell. Give she time.

Jass: Turning back) What? What did you say?

Baba: Whistling ignores him.)

Jass turns to go inside.

The school bell rings. *It is Lunch break.*

Jass gives Baba a big grin. Baba goes to open the school gate. A number of students come into the yard from inside the school. Some sit around the school yard, some exit through the gate.

Enter Vanessa.

Hector: Boy that girl swwwwwwwwwweet!

Jerry : The whole school in love with her. I wish I was in fifth form! I know I would cop it!

Hector and Ossie: *Laugh*) You! Cop that queen over there?!

Vanessa takes a seat under the Mango tree and takes out her lunch. She begins to eat. The boys move nearer to her but not too close.

Enter Nancy.

128

Nancy stands around for a while and then heads over to where Vanessa is sitting. He sits next to her and proceeds to take out his lunch. Vanessa hurriedly picks up her things and exits. Nancy is obviously embarrassed by this. The other students in the yard notice and they all begin to point at Nancy and to laugh! They continue their taunts, getting louder and louder and more menacing.

Enter Miss Richards.

Miss Richards: Ok! Break it up!

The students don't hear her.

Miss Richards: *Raises her voice)* I said enough!

Still the students continue. Baba appears with the school bell and Miss. Richards goes close to a few students and rings the bell close to their ears. This shocks them out of their activity. Several of them leave holding their ears!

Miss Richards: I swear to God ! These students going to make me old before my time!

Baba: You telling me?! It's like the whole bunch of them drink demon blood this weekend and then turn up here to torment people this god-sent Monday morning! You know I had to fix that padlock twice for the morning? Twice?!

Miss Richards: Fix the padlock? Why?

Baba: One a dem pick it to get out and one a dem lash it with a big stone to get in!

Miss Richards: You tell the principal?

Baba: Mr. Bubly?! That poor man got so much to worry about. I don't want to burden him with something else again.

Miss Richards: But he should know these things!

Baba: And what he could do if he know? Nowadays you can't beat these children. Back in my day the headmaster woulda bench them whole pack a dem in they underwear alone in front of the whole school! But now? They do what they want! No respect! No behavior! No nothing! But it can't go on for long!

Miss Richards: Children can be disciplined without beating.

Baba: Yes I know! But these beasts look like they would respond to anything but a whip?

129

Miss Richards: Yes...of course.

Baba: You young yet. Wet behind the ears. You will learn.

Miss Richards: Who are these students who tampered with the locks? I will talk to them.

Baba: Leon Decruz and ....

Miss Richards: Leon picked the lock this morning? Are you sure?

Baba: Why people always questioning my faculties? My eyes and ears are in perfect working condition thank you!

Miss Richards: So it was Leon?

Baba: Yes Leon.

Miss Richards: Was he alone?

Baba: He is the one that pick the lock but was about four of them. That girl who always with him...

Miss Richards: Aha. Samantha....

Baba: And she sidekick Tracy ....

Miss Richards: And of course if Tracy was there then Keith was there....

Baba: Yes! They whole pack of them come in good - good this morning and then turn right around and went back when the last bell ring!

Miss Richards: You know where they went?

Baba: Must be somewhere in some den of iniquity!

Miss Richards: Don't think the worst . They might just have gone to somebody's house.

Baba: Huh! Like I said. You young. You will learn!

Miss Richards: You know I went to teacher's college with Samantha's mother...

Baba: From the way that girl does behave, I didn't think her mother was anybody proper!

Miss Richards: Huh! I'll have to look into this. Thanks Baba.

Baba: Good luck! **Exits.**

Lights Fade to Black.

Scene 3

Lights up on the schoolyard three days later. *Three younger boys are playing basketball. Nancy is looking on. Enter Keith and Jass with Tracy and Susie on the backs of their Bikes. They park the Bikes and regard the game for a moment. Then Keith whispers something to Jass and the two start laughing. They approach the playing boys.*

Keith: Gimme a game ! (*Commands the ball. Bounces it.*)

The players wait around as he dribbles and makes a dunk.

Jass: What?! Boy you could play ! (*Takes the ball.*) But not better than me!

Keith: Ha! (*To the other boys*) How about a game ?

Jass: Yes! Three- a- side!

The other boys try to back off.

Jass: What happen? You all scared ?!

Keith: Points to two of the boys) You all on my team!

The boys are reluctant to join him.

Keith: I said you all on my team! Come!

The boys shuffle over to his side.

Jass: Looks around. There is only one boy left) I guess you on my side.

The boy goes and stands beside Jass.

Jass: But that wouldn't be fair. We need another man.... (*Looks around*) Hmmmmm.... (*Shouts at Nancy*) Hey! Nancy! I need another man for my team....

131

Nancy: No thanks (*Gets up to go inside.*)

Jass: *Running after him and grabbing him*) I said I need you for my team.

Nancy: I can't play basketball.

Keith: Today is a good day to learn! (*Bounces the ball to Nancy.*)

Nancy: No thanks!

Jass: *Yanks him around*) Where you going boy?!

Tracy and Susie gather closer and begin to laugh in a very vulgar fashion.

Keith: You wasting that nice height of yours!

Nancy: Sorry about that!

Jass: *Pushes him roughly*) Boy! Youse get me so mad...look I could....I could ! (*He pushes Nancy really hard and he goes reeling out of control and collides with Vanessa who has just entered the school yard.*)

Nancy ends up on the ground at Vanessa's feet. He looks up at her, hurriedly brushes himself off in embarrassment and hurries off in the direction of the classrooms. Tracy and Susie continue to laugh uproariously. **Vanessa pauses for a while and then exits to the classroom.**

Jass and Keith laugh.

Keith : *To Jass*) He get away this time. But not forever.

Jass: Anyway we got a game to play.

Keith: So what we going to do about the third man for your squad?

Jass: No problem! I could still beat the whole pack of you all with one man short?

Keith: In you dreams!

Jass: You want to bet?

Keith: Sure if you so stupid!

Jass: Deal ! (*They slap palms.*)

Keith: *Pulling out some money. To the boys on his team*) Gimme your money!

Hector: Its my lunch money for the week!

Keith: Don't worry we are about to double it!

Jerry: But suppose we lose!

Keith: Three upon two? We can't lose!

All the boys hesitate and Keith advances upon them menacingly. Reluctantly they give in.

Jass stretches out his hand for the money from Ossie, the boy on his team. The boy gives him the money without a word. Jass hands the money to Keith who counts it all.

Keith: Good we have over two thousand[6]. Winner take all!

Jass: Right!

They begin to play. Keith scores first , then a member of his team scores again then Jass scores and scores again. The game progress for a while until **the bell rings** *while Jass is ahead.*

Jass: That's the class bell. Twenty -seventeen. We win! Bling! Bling! Hand over the money!

Keith: *Very calmly)* Shucks! We lose. (*Hands over the money to Jass. Shrugs at the two boys on his team.*) We lost. Sorry boys!

Hector: But that was my lunch money!!

Jerry: And my bus fare!

The bell rings again.

Keith: The second bell! You all will be late for class....

Keith and Jass exit with Susie and Tracy to the class room leaving the three boys close to tears.

Hector: I going to tell Mr. Bulby too!

Keith: You will just get expelled!

133

Jerry: For what ? We didn't do anything!

Jass: You were gambling in the schoolyard! It's against the rules!

Enter Samantha walking.

Susie and Tracy rush to her.

Susie: Sammy! How come your father drop you to school today? Something happen to Lion?

Samantha: No . He ok.

Tracy: So what happen? You all break up?

Samantha: No!

Susie: So?

Samantha: Some stink mouth person tell my mother how I skipping school and going off with Leon.

Tracy: What? That sad!

Samantha: And my father say I grounded for life plus I can't hang out with Leon anymore!

Susie: What?! They can't do you that!

The Bell rings again. Enter Baba.

Baba: Ok! That was the third bell. All who got places to go, go now because I closing this gate!

Tracy: Like if that ever stop anybody!

Baba: Keep on so! If this one don't stop you the big ones by Camp[7] street will one of these days!

The girls exit to the class room.

Baba padlocks the gate.

Lights up on Miss Richards classroom as the students are being seated.

134

When the lights come up. Nancy is already sitting in his seat near the front of the class.

Enter Vanessa.

Nancy buries his head in his book to avoid meeting her eyes.

Vanessa averts her head and proceeds to sit as far away from him as possible.

Enter Miss Richards.

Miss Richards: Hi Guys!

Vanessa and Nancy: Morning Miss.

Enter Keith, Tracy, Jass, Susie and Samantha.

Miss Richards: Wow! A full class! The sun will shine at midnight tonight!

Jass and Susie sit at the back of the class in their usual seats. Because the seats are arranged three in a row, When Vanessa sits in the second row, there are only two seats available for Samantha, Kevin and Tracy. Kevin and Tracy sit in the second row next to Vanessa. Samantha stands in front of Vanessa and jerks her head in a signal that Vanessa should move. Vanessa ignores her.

Miss Richards. Samantha...please take your seat.

Samantha: It's already taken by this "dry up"[8] girl here!

Miss Richards: There are several other seats available Samantha. Just take one and settle down.

Samantha: She don't sit in this row! This is my seat!

Miss Richards: If you were a regular visitor to this class maybe people would remember where you usually sit.

Samantha: *Tugging at Vanessa)* Girl! Get up I said!

Susie: *Joins in by pushing on the back of Vanessa's chair.)*

Miss Richards: *Gets out of her seat and approaches)* If I have to tell you sit down one more time Samantha, your parents will hear about this!

Susie and Tracy exchange knowing looks. Samantha goes and sits at the back next to Susie.

135

Miss Richards: For those of you who thought it wise to skip the class on Monday morning, we have begun a new topic in literature. (*She drops a book on each of the desks of Samantha, Keith and Tracy*) "The Tales of Anansi"!

Kevin: What! Anansi! Like they think we in first form or what?!

Tracy: Shhhhhhh! Boy you stupidy or what? This going to be the easiest CXC anybody ever write!

Miss Richards: Now I gave some homework last session. It was to read the first chapter. Susie...
Tell us about that first story.

Susie: Miss I....

Miss Richards: Ah ha?

Susie: Miss we had a black-out and I didn't get to read the book.

Miss Richards: Tired excuse. Heard it a million times. Jass?

Jass: The first chapter was the story of how Anansi outsmarted the Tiger.

Miss Richards: *Writes "Outsmarted" on the board*) Good. That's a good word Jass. Outsmarted. What was the plot of the story Vanessa?

Vanessa: Ahm...basically Anansi was walking in the jungle one day when he noticed a Lion standing in front of his house waiting to eat him. So he had to think of a way to get rid of the Lion plus save himself at the same time....

Nancy: So he came up with a brilliant plan !

Vanessa: *Shoots him a nasty look*) Stop butting in! I wasn't finished!

Nancy: Sorry.

Vanessa: Miss, continue?

Miss Richards: By all means....

Vanessa: So Anansi devised a brilliant plan!

Samantha: Copy cat!

Vanessa: It's in the book! If you all could even read!

136

Samantha: Girl you pushing your luck with me....

Miss Richards: The whole pack of you all pushing your luck with life! Settle down and focus! This exam is a month away!

Keith: What's the difference? Every body going to fail anyway!

Vanessa: Speak for yourself!

Tracy: He right! Nobody from this school don't pass no *literature*!

Miss Richards: Well someday somebody going to change that and I hope it's going to be one of you!

Tracy: My mother say that literature is a pack nonsense! Nobody can't make money off of learning that or nothing!

Miss Richards: Then I hope you don't grow up to be as ignorant as your mother!

Tracy: Miss!! You telling me about my mother?!!

Miss Richards: No you were telling the class what she said. I am saying that I hope that you will know a little more a bout the importance of literature in life, unlike your mother!

Tracy: Everybody here , heard *you* call *my mother* ignorant!

Miss Richards: *Picks up the dictionary from her desk. She hands it to Tracy)* Find the word ignorant, young lady and read the meaning to the class. (*She turns to the board and writes the word "Ignorant".)*

Tracy thumbs through the dictionary and finds the word.

Tracy: *Reading)* Ohhhhhhh.........

Miss Richards: Read it aloud please.

Tracy: Ignorance...misinformed or lacking in knowledge.

Miss Richards: So you still think I was insulting your mother?

Tracy: I though you was saying that she was stupid.

Miss Richards: *Taking the dictionary back)* No. But you see if you used to read more, you would understand the shades of differences between words. That is

137

one of the important things about learning literature. It allows you to read and understand things that you would not come into contact with in your own life.

Vanessa: Miss could we get back to the story now? I wasn't finished !

Miss Richards: Sorry Vanessa. Continue.

Vanessa: So Anansi had to find a way to get this big, hungry Lion from in front his house. So he thought about it and thought about it ....

Samantha: And thought about it!

Jass: Ok we get the picture. He thought about it a lot!

Vanessa: Yes! And then he came up with a plan...

Keith: Well hurry up nuh girl and tell us what the plan was nuh!

Vanessa: So Anansi, went looking in the forest until he came across the skeleton of a dead elephant. And then he dragged the skeleton close enough to where the Lion could hear him and then he started to holler loud! " Oh! That was a juicy elephant! But now I hungry again, yes! Today, I feeling to eat a nice juicy Lion..." Well the Lion heard this and saw the elephant carcass and really believing that Anansi could eat him he ran away and .....

Samantha: The tinin bend .....

All: And the story end!

Susie: *Rising and pretending to conduct the class*) Tantanatan-tan-tan!

Miss Richards: *Laughs*) You see ! Literature can be fun! Now....there are a few things about this story that are important for us to discuss. This first is the word that Jass so brilliantly gave us this morning "outsmart".

Keith and Jass High five.

Miss Richard: Now did Anansi really outsmart the Lion? Yes or no? Those who say yes raise their hand ?

All raise their hands.

Miss Richards: Ok. Well then, how did he do this?

Susie: By using the coconut[9] that God give him!

138

Miss Richards: Very good Susie! But I really wish you wouldn't use your own words to describe things. On the exam the people marking will have to understand what you mean and everybody will not know that when you say "coconut" you mean the head or brain. Try to remember that ok. But that was a good answer! And why do you think he had to use his brain?

Nancy: Cause he was a spider!

Jass: So?

Tracy: A spider is a little tiny thing!

Keith: So ?

Samantha: A spider can't fight a Lion and win!

Enter Leon:

Lyon: Sure right about that! (*Gives Miss Richards a big grin*) Good morning Miss Richards!

Miss Richards: Must be a good morning for you to show up here. Late but better late than never!

Leon looks for a place to sit but all the places in the back of the room are filled so he sits in front next to Nancy.

Samantha immediately gets up and joins him.

Susie: Eh! Is just so we get bus off!

Miss Richards: *Handing Leon a book*) Nice to see you Leon.

Lyon: My name is Lion.

Miss Richards: L-E-O-N. Means Leon in this class. You can call yourself whatever you want outside! (*To class*) Great! Somebody put all those great thoughts in a sentence for me. Nancy?

Nancy: Ahm......let's see...because Anansi could not win a physical fight with Lion he had to use his brain to win?

Miss Richards: Yes that's it! And so what would be the moral of this story Susie?

Susie: Ahm..........

Vanessa: Where there's a will there is a way!

The Bell Rings.

Miss Richards: That's right. Even in the face of mighty odds, you can prevail if you use your head! See you all next week folks! Read chapter two for homework!

All groan loudly.

The lights fade to Black.

Scene 4

The same day. Lunch break. Lights up on the schoolyard.

Leon walks over to his motor bike and kick starts it.

Leon: *To Samantha*) Let's buss it![10]

Samantha: Leon....

Leon: Lion!

Samantha: Lion...I can't....

Leon: You can't? Can't ?! When you learn that word!

Samantha: Since my father and mother find out I was cutting school!

Leon: Find out? How?!

Samantha: Somebody told Miss Richards and she is my mother's good friend!

Leon: Miss Richards tell your mother? But how she know?

Samantha: I don't know. My mother said reliable sources....

Leon: You got any idea is who?

Samantha: I have my suspicions....

Leon: Like who?

Samantha: I don't know for sure and I don't want to cause any problems....

Leon: Girl ! Tell me who...

Samantha: I think is Jass and Susie!

Leon: Jass and Susie? My Jass and Susie? No! They would never betray me!

Samantha: Well it can't be Keith and Tracy because they were doing the same thing as we!

Lyon: But it could be somebody else....

Samantha: Like who?

Leon: Anyone of the other students.

Samantha: You know they too 'fraid you for that! Is dem. That girl Susie never like me!

Leon: That is dung!

Samantha: She want me out of the way so she could be the one riding with you!

Leon: Now that's pure jealousy! But I like it!

Samantha: Is true!

Leon: I going to get to the bottom of this ! Wait and see and then whoever it is will know never to mess with Leon the Lion again!

Samantha: In the meantime I grounded for life!

Leon: What?! So you can't come to lunch with me?

Samantha: My parent's don't even want me to talk to you anymore!

Lyon: So what? Screw dem!

Samantha: What?

Lyon: That's what I say! Screw dem! You and me going to do we own thing anyway!

Samantha : This is serious Le....Lion! I can't take the risk. If I don't show up for every class everyday Miss Richards going to tell my mother and then I will be in

141

big trouble! Plus my father coming to drop me and pick me up everyday! They have me like I in a prison!

Leon: So me and you done then?

Samantha: What?!

Leon: If you can't hang with me....we can't be together. It won't make no sense.

Samantha: But you're my boy Lion! It's just for a while...what my parent's say. We could wait a while till they trust me again and then things will get back to normal....

Leon: Girl look! You know I never wait on anything my whole life....

Samantha: But is me...Samantha....your girl....

Leon: All I have to tell you is you either with me or your with your parents!

Samantha: But they will put me out if I don't do what they say...

Leon: And I will cut you off if you don't do what I say!

Samantha: That's not fair!

Leon: You got one day to make up your mind about this, you hear?

Samantha: But you said you loved me?

Leon: I can't love you if I can't be with you girl! Get real! (*Kiss her on her cheek and rides off with a flourish.*)

Samantha: Leon wait! Please...

Enter Keith, Jass, Tracy and Susie and Nancy.

Nancy is bouncing a basketball around under the mango tree.

Tracy: Sammy, you coming to lunch or what?

Susie: You forget the girl grounded?

Sammy: Why you do it Susie? Why you tell Miss Richards?

Susie: Me?! I didn't tell nobody! You keep secret for me and I keep your for you!

142

Sammy: Then Jass is you!

Jass: Girl don't be stupid!

Sammy: You always frighten and don't want to come with us. Had to be you!

Jass: Look! I didn't tell anybody anything. Could be anybody!

Sammy: These other kids too scared of Leon to squeal on him....

Keith: Except that crazy boy.... Nancy....

Tracy: Nancy? He is the most scared of all. He even let Vanessa bully him! Naw! I think is one of the two of you or both!

Keith: My father always say " your best friend could be your worst enemy."

Jass: That was Bob Marley!

Samantha: Look Shut up! Just shut up!

Jass: Hey? What's up with that?

Samantha: You lucky Leon ain't here now...otherwise he'd make you bleed!

Susie: So we said we didn't tell ok! Is true so cool it!

Samantha: And you....as to you? You talk my business...we will see how you like it when I do the same to you! (*Walks off.*)

Susie: Samantha! It wasn't me!

Samantha: *Calling over her shoulder*) Don't worry. I know you man hungry since you was a baby!

Susie: *Turns pale and sits down.*)

Jass: Susie ! You ok?

Tracy: Guilty conscience! (*Flounces off.*)

Keith follows her.

Jass: Susie.....

Susie: *Hugging her knees*) Get away from me Jass! Just get away from me!

143

Jass: But....

Susie: *Pushes him away roughly*) You might as well go now! Because soon you wouldn't want to know me!

Jass: No. I am never going to say I don't know you...

Susie: My life is over. She is going to tell.

Jass: Then we have to stop her!

Susie: Stop her? How?!

Jass: I don't know. Cut out her tongue?

Susie: What?!

Jass: I was joking. Just trying to make you laugh!

Susie: That's not funny!

Jass: Ok. Look we going to find a way ok. But you to tell me what's wrong ok? You have to tell me...

Susie: *Nods.*)

Enter Baba whistling.

Lights fade to Black.

Scene 5

8. 30 am the following Monday morning. Lights up on the school. It is deserted except for Baba, puttering around the yard.

Enter Leon. *He looks around and parks his bike quietly, and the walks back up the road and stands watching just off.*

Enter Vanessa. *She waves to someone off and then starts towards the school yard. Leon jumps out from his hiding place and begins to follow her.*

Leon: I know you had to have a man!

144

Vanessa: What?!

Leon: All this time you playing miss "hoity toity"[11] and fooling everybody. But I catch you fair, you can't fool me!

Vanessa: Look boy get out of my face!

Leon: Is not your face I want to be in.....

Vanessa: *Does not respond but keeps walking briskly.)*

Leon: *Grabbing her arm)* I see you Saturday night at the dance. I could not believe my eyes! Girl you were the bomb[12]!

Vanessa: So, you think a person can't party and still be decent?

Leon: But you had a banna[13] you was dancing with all night! Tight!

Vanessa: So ?

Leon: Is the same banna just drop you off ?! He can't handle a girl like you! You deserve more!

Vanessa: *Laughs.)*

Leon: I serious. You deserve me!

Vanessa: Boy look! Never! Never- ever- never!

Leon: You just talking! Look. Is a long time I like you. I telling you this. I love you! I never tell this to any other girl!

Vanessa: *Laughing)* Really? Well don't waste it on me.

Leon: Look! I am Lion ! King of the jungle! I could get any girl I want!

Vanessa: Not me!

They reach the classroom. Lyon enters behind Vanessa who sits in her usual position and opens her book.

Leon: *Leans over her desk)* I like you! I mean it! And I will get you at any cost!

Vanessa: Look! I have to finish reading this chapter before Miss Richards gets here ok.

Leon: But I not finish talking to you!

Vanessa: I finish with you though! What you think I would do with you? You can't even read properly and you don't have the good sense to try to learn? Instead what you do? You cut school and try to play you so cool. Nothing cool about being a fool!

Leon: What? ! Who you talking to like that?!

Vanessa: Only me and you in this room....

Leon: *Grabbing her)* Say you're sorry!

Vanessa: Let me go boy!

Leon: Ok. You insult me! I will insult you (*Tries to kiss her.*)

They struggle.

Enter Nancy.

Nancy: Leon what are you doing!?

Leon: What it look like I doing? (*Tries to kiss her again.*)

Vanessa: Stop it!

Nancy: Well...I know ....but she says to stop!

Leon: I will stop when I want.

Vanessa: Look! Leon get your hands off me! You idiot!

Nancy: Leon. I think you should stop that, ok!

Leon: Or else what ? You little *vanskinnymite*[14]!

Nancy: Or else I will have to stop you!

Leon: *Continues to hold on to Vanessa)* Yeah right!

Nancy: Boy ....I...I telling you to stop! Desist ! Now!

Enter Samantha. *She sees Lyon and turns away.*

146

Leon: *Ignores Nancy.)*

Enter Jass and Susie.

Nancy picks up a big book and whacks Leon really hard on the head with it.

Jass moves forward to hit Nancy but Susie restrains him.

Leon turns around and sees them. Rubbing his head, lets go of Vanessa and turns on Nancy) You dead boy! Dead here today!

Enter Miss Richards.

Miss Richards: Good Morning all!

Leon restrains himself and takes his seat at the back of the class. Vanessa straightens herself out and sits near the front next to Nancy.

Vanessa: *To Nancy)* Thanks! But he's going to get you for that!

Nancy: Don't worry. I have it covered.

Jass and Susie go to sit next to Leon but he stops them with a crude sign and waves them away.

Jass and Susie move their seats so that they are across the room and as far away as possible from Leon.

Enter Samantha. *She goes to sit next to Leon but with her back to him.*

Miss Richards: Nice to see you all so nice a early this Monday! I hope you all had a nice weekend and that you did my homework!

Vanessa: Yes Miss!

Miss Richards: I take it that only Vanessa did the homework?

The rest of the class protest that is not the case.

Enter Keith and Tracy. *They move the chairs so they can sit with Leon . The class now is*
arranged in a way that shows a clear division between Leon's crew and the others.

147

Miss Richards: Ok then. Since you all were so studious this weekend, can anybody tell me which of these folk tales explains how Anansi, the spider came to have a bald head and to hide among tall grass and trees?

Vanessa: *Puts up her hand.)*

Miss Richards: Not you yet. Anyone else who said they did the homework. I am going to spin my pen on this desk and whoever it points to you answer (*She spins.)*

Susie: *Under her breath)* This woman is nuts!

Miss Richards: And the lucky person is Susie!

Susie: Me? ...

Jass: *Whispers to her.)*

Susie: Ah... it was the story of Anansi's Hat Shaking Dance !

Miss Richards: Go on. Tell us the story...

Susie: Tell?! Ahm...well Anansi had this hat that used to do a little dance...

Miss Richards: Aha?

Susie: ...And then he lost the hat and then he lost his hair because the sun in Africa was too hot!

Nancy: Really?

Samantha: *Begins to laugh)* She's making it up! True to form!

Susie: Oh shut up!

Miss Richards: You know Susie, you have such a good imagination. I only wish you would put it to good use.

Jass: Miss ....

Lyon: Punk!

Jass: At least I could read!

Miss Richards: That is enough! Jass we are listening....

Jass: The story of how Anansi became bald is called Anansi and the Hat Shaking dance. Basically, Anansi was trying to show off how long he could do without eating at his mother- in- laws wake. But the hunger overtook him and he stole some beans to eat. But then his friends came in the room and the only place he could find to hide the hot beans fast enough was under his top hat!

Miss Richards: Great Jass! Congratulations. Next person...Keith what is the connection with the name of the story, Anansi's baldness and the hat?

Keith: Me Miss?

Susie: Miss that's the dunce side of the room!

Samantha: No way! Miss I know! The story is called the Hat Shaking Dance because as the hot beans was burning his head under the hat , Anansi was shaking his head from side to side to cool off!

Leon: Rising and demonstrating) Yes! Like this!

His side of the class laughs. The others remain silent.

Samantha: Yes! Like that! And when his friends asked him why he was doing that, he said that it was a new hat shaking dance that he had learned!

Tracy: Anansi was really deceptive!

Samantha: Like some people in this room! (Casts a look at Susie, who looks away.)

Miss Richards: There is another part of the story. When the hat falls off and Anansi's friends see his burnt head and the beans what happens?

Vanessa: He bows his head in shame and asks the grass to hide him from sight!

Miss Richards: Right and what is the moral of this story?

Lyon: Don't let your friends find out your business (Gives an evil sign to Jass and Susie.)

Miss Richards: Maybe. But what about Anansi....Susie...what does it say about Anansi and what lesson does it teach?

Susie: About showing off, lying and hiding things... it's got a price.

Miss Richards: Yes!

Samantha: Well she ought to know ! She good at all of that!

Susie: Girl get off my back!!

Samantha: Me? Is your father you shoulda tell that!

There is a shocked silence.

Then Susie rises and lounges for Samantha. Miss Richards gets in between and holds them back.

Miss Richards: Girls! Girls!

Susie: Sobs.)

Jass: Susie.....

Susie: I know she woulda talk.....

Jass: But you did something about it...you did something!

Miss Richards: Ok. The rest of you go to the library and continue reading. Susie I need to talk to you...,

Leon rises and shows Nancy the sign of a gun to his head.

Vanessa: Ah! Miss... could me and Nancy stay here at the back of the class? We will be real quiet...

Miss Richards: I really prefer to ....

Leon: *Passing close to Nancy and Vanessa)* You could run but yuh can't hide! Outside!

Miss Richards: *Looks at him and then at Nancy and Vanessa)* Oh! Ok.....But mind your business!
(She motions to Susie to sit at her desk) So what was that about?

Susie is silent.

Miss Richards: Listen! Not so long ago I was a teenager too...so what was that about?

Susie: *Sobs.)*

Miss Richards: Susie ...please talk to me....I want to help..

Susie: Miss...Miss you wouldn't understand....

Miss Richards: Was your father ...was he ...touching you?

Susie: *Nods.)*

Miss Richards: I see. We need to call the police....

Susie: I called them! I called the Police! Now he is in jail and It's all your fault!

Miss Richards: Me?!

Susie: You had to go and let us read those stories ! You had to make us think about things we didn't want to think! Yes! It was your fault!

Miss Richards: Susie...please....you did the right thing by calling the Police.

Susie: But all these years ! I did nothing! Cried myself to sleep, bowed my head in shame and I did nothing!

Miss Richards: You were young and afraid Susie...it's an awful position to be in. It's not your fault. None of it! Believe that!

Susie: But Anansi say...no matter who small and weak you might be, you could defend your self...you have to open your voice and tell ...and I toll...I toll Samantha ...and I tell the Police and.....oh Miss Richards! Oh! *(Breaks down.)*

Miss Richards: *Folds the Susie in her arms and rocks her.)* Shhhhhh! He was a bad man and you did right to defend yourself.Shhhhhhhh!

Susie: What's going to happen to me now eh Miss? Now everybody know?

Miss Richards: Ahhhhhhhh! It's going to be hard on you. But you have to be strong.

Susie: Jass...Jass going to hate me!

Miss Richards: Maybe. But he may love you enough to still be your friend.

Susie: You think so?

Miss Richards: Aha. And if not you can always count on me...anyday, anytime....

Susie: *Sobs.)*

Miss Richards: Susie…Susie. Life is full of sad stories and happy stories. But they don't write themselves. We write them. Sometimes we can make a story that starts sad have a happy end. It's hard and I know you feel like you're dying now…but you could change your story…just imagine a wonderful end….

Susie: Sighs.)

Miss Richards: Come! Wipe your eyes and put on a bright face. I will walk with you to your next class, ok?

Susie: Next class Miss? ! I….

Miss Richards: Yes, you're going to go and then we can take it from there, ok?

Susie: Hesitates but rises.)

They Exit.

Vanessa: If we don't think of something both me and you dead!

Nancy: Look ! It's ok….

Vanessa: Look Nancy. You don't have to impress me. I am already impressed by what you did this morning and the way you conduct yourself. But this is a serious thing. Leon is crazy and violent….

Nancy: I know.

Enter Baba. He cleans the board.

Vanessa: Plus people saw him take the blow. He was embarrassed. He will want to get back at you in the worst way.....

Nancy: Sighing) I wish he would just disappear....

Vanessa: Well he's not about to do that!

Nancy: Turning to Baba) Hey Baba!

Baba: What?

Nancy: Suppose you had to defeat a big bully and you was a skinny person, what you would do?

Baba: Huh! All this energy people spend on you- all and still nothing don't stick eh? All this literature you read and analyze? You can't think up a solution? You have to ask me?

Vanessa: We just thought that ....

Baba: Because I am a Janitor I must have been a bad john when I was young?

Vanessa: No.

Baba: *Walks over to them and picks up the Anansi book)* Hmmmmm. Nice book. Anansi eh?
I guess if you are a little skinny man and you have to fight off a big hulk of a man ....you have to be spider man!!! (*Laughs and Exits.*)

Vanessa: He thinks this is funny!

Nancy: *Is thumbing through the book.*)

Vanessa: Nancy! You can't be reading at a time like this? We have to go outside just now! Leon will be waiting.....

Nancy: *Engrossed)* Shhhh! Wait......

Vanessa: Nancy!

Nancy: *Laughing)* That it! (*Laughs some more*) I have it! I have it ! (*Laughs again.*)

Lights fade with his laughter.

Scene 6

Lunch time that same day. The lunch bell rings. Enter the three boys into the school yard.

Hector: I ain't going to lunch today!

Jerry: Neither me!

Ossie: Yes, I hear they going to pashway[15]!

153

Enter Leon swaggering. *He saunters over to his bike, pushes it to the gate and blocks the gateway. Then he perches himself on the seat and calmly waits.*

Samantha enters and goes over to him.

Samantha: Leon.

Lyon: Lion!

Samantha: Lion! I just found out. Is not Jass and Susie who tell Miss Richards about us.

Lyon: So?

Samantha: So. You don't need to do them anything Ly....Lion....

Lyon: Too bad. I just feel like beating up some people today! (*Pulls out a knife from his pocket.*)

Samantha: Oh my god! Leon ! No!

Lyon: *Pushes her away*) Plus is not really Jass and them I after right now....

Samantha: Leon. It's not worth it....you will go to jail.

Leon: I don't care!

Samantha: That is stupid!

Leon: Girl! Move from here before you get some too!

Samantha backs off.

Enter Vanessa. She sees Leon at the gate and crosses directly to him.

Vanessa: Hi !

Leon: I ain't ready for you yet! Where your hero from this morning?

Vanessa: *Laughing*) Who Nancy? He could ever be my hero? A nerd like that?!

Leon: He hiding nuh?

Vanessa: What you think?

Leon: Damn headmaster wouldn't come out the canteen, otherwise I deal with him right in there!

Vanessa: You look so strong today? You been lifting weights recently?

Leon: *Flexing*) Nah! Natural muscle. Feel....

Vanessa: *Rubs her hands on his shoulders*) Hmmmmmmm. That's power boy! But maybe you just big so and you not strong!

Leon: What you mean?

Vanessa: You might be big but not fit.

Leon: I am Lion! I strong and fit !

Vanessa: So why you need a knife to fight that skinny little Nancy?

Leon: I don't *need* it.

Vanessa: Really? People might think so...

Leon: Well I don't need it. I could beat him with my little finger!(*Puts the knife back in his pocket.*)

Vanessa: So when you going to lunch?

Leon: You just want to get me away from this gate. You think I stupid?

Vanessa: I know better than that! But if you going to take me to lunch you will have to move?

Leon: You to lunch?

Vanessa: Aha!

Leon: Another day. After I take care of business.

Vanessa: Whatever you say.

Enter Jass and Susie. *They spot Leon by the gate and do not advance any further.*

Leon: Cowards!

Enter Nancy. *He is carrying a large two by four.*

155

Leon: *Steps off his bike at the sight of it and doubles over laughing)* I don't believe it! Nancy and a two by four ! To beat me ! Haaaaaaaa!

Nancy: Hey Lion! That's what you call yourself right?!

Leon: That's right, fine boy!

Nancy: And you so big and bad that you could beat anybody right?

Leon: So people say!

Nancy: Suppose I beat you here today?

Leon: *Laughs)* Suppose your nose was a door post!

Nancy: Seriously....

Leon: If you could even land one punch on me before I drop you! I would say you good and give you anything you want!

Nancy: Anything?

Leon: Anything!

Nancy: Ok.

Leon: You not only maaga[16] but you crazy!

Everyone in the school yard is silent. Nancy approaches slowly as Leon advances. The students gather round .

Nancy swings the two by four the first time and misses.

Leon: Miiiis!! (*He continues to advance.)*

Nancy swings again and misses again.

Leon swings at Nancy and lands a punch. Kicks into boxing mode.

Nancy swings again.
Leon grabs the plank with both hands and yanks it away from Nancy. He laughs as Nancy retreats. He attempts to drop the plank to get to his knife but finds that he can't drop it plank.

Nancy stands quietly watching him.

156

Leon: What the hell? You put contact cement on this wood boy? !

Leon tries to swing at Nancy with the plank but because his hands are stuck to it he can't control it and he over balances.

Nancy quickly walks over to him and straddles him in a wrestlers lock.

Vanessa: *Steps forward*) See I told you. I prefer brains over brute force any day! (*Counting*) One....

Lyon struggles in vain to throw Nancy off.

The other students : Two....three.... You lose Lyon!

Nancy: *Still sitting on Lyon*) You lose. And I get anything I want....

Lyon: No! You cheat....

Vanessa: Nah! This game had no rules. Was plain win or lose.

Nancy: Don't tell me you planning to go back on your word now?

The other students begin to taunt Lyon: You promise the man who win will get anything etc., etc.

Lyon: *Looks around and decides to try and safe face*) I bigger than that man! What you want?

Nancy: No more fighting. After today, this story between me and you done!

Hector: *Steps forward*) And you have to stop bullying we for we lunch money!

Jerry and Ossie: We too!

Lyon: *Groans*) Anybody else?!

Samantha: And you have to stop hitting on every girl you see!

Lyon: I agree to everything else except that.

Nancy: Deal?

Lyon: *Groans)* Yeah... yeah.

Nancy: Sorry we can't shake hands on that man (*Walks off.*)

157

Vanessa: Nancy! Nancy! Wait! That was brilliant! Great!

Nancy: Yeah!

Vanessa: How you think that up boy?

Nancy: Chapter 5. How Anansi Got the Sky God's Stories. He used his brain to catch a Leopard, a fairy, some Maribuntas[17] and a big Camoudi snake. You should read it sometime.

Vanessa: Wow! And that actually worked! I thought he was going to kill you!

Nancy: Nah!

Vanessa: Where you going for lunch ? I could come with you?

Nancy: *Laughs)* For real?

Vanessa: Yes!

Nancy and Vanessa Exit.

Hector: That Nancy real bright boy!

Ossie: Imagine! Fight done and not one punch land!

Jerry: And look he gone with we girl !

Hector, Ossie and Jerry Exit.

Enter Baba. Sees Samantha and Keith and Tracy helping Lyon up and trying to pry the plank from his hands.

Baba: Huh! Binding cement from the industrial arts department . Very, very strong. *(Takes a pull at the plank but it wont budge.)* Huh! I don't think this will come off like that! *(Pulls out an electric saw)* Might have to cut the hands off the plank...

Lyon shrieks and all the others freeze upon hearing that.

Baba: *Laughing heartily as he advances)* ..... But then again I might just leave you there to think about life for a few days! *(Stripping off his janitors clothes. Bows to the audience)* And so my mission here is finished. Anansi say the tinin bend and the story end! (*He laughs heartily.)* **Exits**

Light fades to black.

The End.

Glossary of Terms for Anansi's Way

[1] The moon runs until day catches up with it/ things always have to change.

[2] Diss = disrespect.

[3] Gwan = go on.

[4] Cockish = wily, someone who is dishonest.

[5] Fine = very skinny, slender.

[6] Guyana dollar equivalent of US $35.

[7] Refers to the maximum security state prison at Camp Street, Georgetown.

[8] Dry up = skinny/ very thin.

[9] Cocount = head/brain.

[10] Buss it = leave the place.

[11] Hoity toity = uppity/ above reproach/ saint like.

[12] "Were the bomb" = you were looking really fabulous, you were exceptional.

[13] Banna = boy/man/male.

[14] Vanskinnymite = really skinny and small person.

[15] Pashway = big fight.

160

[16] Maaga = really skinny.

[17] Marabuntas = stinging wasps.

A Fair Maids Tale
A Play in One Act
Paloma Mohamed

Fairmaid (Faymaid) - Female water spirit, half woman and half fish like a Mermaid. Beautiful with long hair which she combs with a silver or golden comb. Finding the comb can bring great riches or death. Fairmaids can change into full women. They lure men into the water sometimes taking them to live underwater or sometimes killing them. Also known as Water Mama, Water Moma or Fai'maid.

Running time: 45 to 60 minutes.

The Characters:

1. Bush Dai-Dai : Protector of the forest
2. Kanima/ Growling Tiger
3. Green Fern: heroine, Fairmaid
4. Billowing Smoke: Green Ferns Grandfather and village Piaiman
5. Brown Sapling – Billowing Smoke's wife.
6. Yellow Morning: Green Fern's mother
7. Red Dust: Green Fern's father
8. Mako: The Great Spirit Makoniama
9. Eagle Head: Man in the Village
10. Grey Thunder: Man in the village
11. Little Snake : Boy
12. Blue Parrot: Boy
13. Shaking Arrow: Boy
14. Gentle Breeze: Girl
15. Waking Sun: Girl
16. Two boys for the canoe.
17. Villagers :This play can support as many extra's as possible.

The Setting: A remote Amerindian village in Guyana, maybe in Essequibo, maybe the Rupunini. The lighting is shadowy as sunlight filtering through a canopy of trees. There is constant ambient sound of Crickets, Macaws, Monkeys and wind.

The Set: Towering mountains almost touching the clouds in background. One needs to be functional. Tall forest trees in the foreground. At stage left, a deep running black water river. A few hewn canoes are seen on the bank. At extreme stage right an Amerindian village, represented by a benab or two.

Scene 1

Late evening. Dim light. A canoe being paddled by two young men suddenly capsizes. They scream out " Fairmaid! Help! It's the Fairmaid!" Then they disappear under the water. Eerie flute music is heard as bright light floods the stage.

Dai-Dai: *Calling*) Ay Mako? Mako you there? You listening to me?

164

Sound of rustling in the bush.

Dai-Dai: Ay. I know you there. Always there!

Loud Laughter.

Dai-Dai: *Spins around)* Eh! Eh!

Laughter again. Dai-Dai listens and follows in the direction from which it comes.

Enter a group of young men in their teens. *They are carrying bows, arrows and cutlasses. They are crawling on their bellies and giggling while seeming to stalk something.*

Dai watches them closely as they pass by.

Dai: *Whistling a particular whistle)* Wheooooooo-Wheooooooo-Wheo-Wheo!

There is more rustling in the bush.

The young men fall silent.

Dai Shuffles over to a tree, puts her ear against the trunk and listens, while nodding her head from time to time. She whistles again.

Intense shuffling in the bushes is heard.

Enter Green Fern crawling on her belly and following the trail left by the males.

Dai watches her pass and chuckles in delight.

The lights become dim.

Dai: *Stops laughing and draws in a deep breath)* So you there alright eh, Mako? What you going to show we now? What? It ain't you? Eh! No!? How I coulda make a mistake like that?!! (*She hustles off into the bush. A loud crash is heard followed by a thud. Loud shuffling and another thud.)*

Enter the young men running and shrieking. They exit in the direction of the village.

Green Fern huddles in a corner and tries to hide herself, but it is obvious that whatever is approaching has her cornered. She closes her eyes tightly and waits.

Green Fern: Great Spirit Makoniama. Here is Green Fern. If I am to return to the mountain in the sky today, let me be brave and guide me on my way.

Dai: *Bends down listening to the earth*) Eh! *Now* you talking to me? Because you want me do something for you?!! Well what *you* plan to do for *me*, eh Mako? What?!! (*Listens again*) Ok. Ok. (*Bustles over to Green Fern and covers her with her greenery. The girl is now totally hidden from view.*)

Enter Kanima at great speed. *He is checked as he sees Dai covering the girl. He stops so suddenly that he skids and ends up somersaulting over Dai and the girl. Dai immediately turns to face him.*

Kanima: This is not between me and you Dai-Dai....

Dai: Then you better go you way Kanima, if me and you don't have no business today.

Kanima: You in my way.

Dai: Go 'way. You can't take nothing that belong to me. You know that.

Kanima: What you talking about?

Dai: The girl.

Kanima: You jurisdiction is bush, fish and snake! Not people (*Advances toward Dai.*)

Dai: You right. But this is a technical one....

Kanima: Look is just a magga[i] girl child. Nobody going to miss she....(*Attempts to grab the girl but Dai dodges and the girl dodges with her so they are both able to avoid Kanima.*)

Kanima: *Roars like a Lion*) I got a beast in my belly and it demand flesh nowwwwwwwwww! (*Roars again.*)

Dai: Look for something else nah....

Kanima: I want the girl! *That* girl!

Dai: What about some nice big fish? Yes! The biggest Arapaima's in the Amazon?!

166

Kanima: You trying to feed a Jaguar fish?!

Dai: If it good for Pussy Cat, why not for Tiger Cat?!

Kanima: *Jumps up and down angrily and roars again.)*

Dai: *Starts)* Ahye! My ears!

Green Fern: Covers her ears.)

Dai: But how you expect this maaga child to feed a big cat like you? She so small, only bones really!

Kanima: *Takes a swipe at Dai but she ducks.)*

Dai: Is another reason why you want this *particular* girl eh? You ent' hungry one bit!!! Is her *life* you want! Not her flesh!!!

Kanima: And what you care?!

Dai: The girl ... *technically* belong to me.

Kanima: You?!! *(Laughs).* Which part of you tree bark she pass out? Which part of she is green sap and vine? Or like she have fish tail somewhere and we can't see?

Dai: I was there when Makoniama create she. Red Dust and Yellow Morning lay together right here in this same bush. Under me just like the child lying down now. And when the earth under me start to shake, I know they was going to have a baby, cause the great spirit was sighing so loud. When Yellow Morning was ready to pass the child into this world, she come back right here, by this bush. She alone with the bursting belly. But I was with she all the time. And when the baby was born, I cradle her, even before her own mother and father. And I whisper to she, she name, Green Fern...Green Fern. She was born under me. She is mine.

Kanima: *Crouching low and growling dangerously)* Give - me- the - girl Bush Dai-Dai! You don't know who you protecting and you don't want to cross *me*! Give me she!!!

Dai: *Casting her eyes to the sky and shouting out)* Look Mako! The cat right ! I make to protect leafy things and water things. I don't know how to deal with this girl here who don't have no fins, no roots and no wings!

Mens voices are heard in the distance.

167

Kanima: *Backing away.)* You win for the moment. But you can't protect her forever. *(Shows his fangs and melts into the forest.)*

Green Fern : *Emerging from under Dai. Touches her feet in reverence.)* Jungle Mother thank you! You spread your leaves so wide to cover me! You plant your root so deep to give me strength! You saved me!

Dai: I take my instructions from the big man himself! I don't know *what* he see in this maaga child!

Enter Red Dust , followed by Billowing Smoke, Eagle Head, Grey Thunder and the young boys .

Red Dust: Where?! Where you all see it ?

Little Snake: It was right there. Just back there!

Eagle Head: *Listening to the ground and sniffing the air)* Smell like it nearby here....

Dai Whistles.)

Red Dust: You hear something?!

Dai whistles again.)

Red Dust: Oh! There she is! Green Fern! Why do you *always* wander off like this?!!! The other girls are learning to make Cassareep and you are out here skylarking!!!!

Green Fern: Sorry Papa Red Dust!.

Billowing Smoke: You must not do this, Green Fern. There are things out here, that brave men can't deal with, far less a young girl like you. Promise me you will stop it. One of these days, you might not come back!!!

Green Fern: *Bows her head.)*

Red Dust: You have to start behaving like a girl!

The young boys begin to giggle.

Green Fern: *(To the boys)* Oh shut up! *(Stalks off.)*

Red Dust: Green Fern! You see you are doing it again! Off in the forest by yourself....

He hurries after his daughter. The others follow him except Billowing Smoke.

Billowing Smoke stops a while to examine the earth upon which Kanima had been stamping. He sniffs it and shakes his head.

Billowing Smoke: Hmmmm. Hmmmmmmmm. (Collects some of the earth. Wraps it in a leaf and ties the leaf with a vine which he hangs around his neck.) **Exits.**

Dai: *Lets out a huge sigh of relief)* Ayyyyyyyyyyyyyyyyyyy! Kanima ! I thought he woulda finish me today!!! This kind of stressful work is not for me . No! (*Sighs again).* Look Mako....I do what you ask me. You promise me rain for a week. Now send it!!

There is the sound of thunder and sound of rain.

Dai: Ayyyyyyyy! Yesssssssssssss! Come down and swell the rivers! Come down and bath the dry earth! Come down and wash the mountain tops! Come caress my green children! Come satisfy me! Come!

The figure of Kanima is seen climbing up a short mountain. He reaches the summit and stands surveying the area below him menacingly

Kanima: You didn't win Makoniama! You didn't win ! (*Lets out an loud enraged roar.)*

There is another clap of thunder. Dead Black Out.

Scene 2

The next day. The river bank. Men and boys are pulling in canoes after a fishing trip.

Red Dust: Fiftieth day and no fish!

Eagle Head: Not one!

Grey Thunder: It's like the fish went somewhere else!

Billowing Smoke: Hmmmmmmmm!

Grey Thunder: Hmmmmmmm?! What hmmmmmmmm supposed to mean?!

Eagle Head: Don't harass the old man....

Grey Thunder: *He* is *the Piaiman*. I'm not harassing him. He *supposed* to provide answers. And to me "hhhhhhhhhhmmmmmmm" is not an answer! *(Strides off.)*

Eagle Head: *To Billowing Smoke)* Sorry...

Billowing Smoke: Hmmmmmmmmmm.

Red Dust: We will have to catch more game, or the village will starve.

Growling Tiger: More animals?!! But we almost hunt them to extinction already!

Eagle Head: True. Mostly only babies left. If we kill the young for food before they can have babies of their own, soon there will be no animals left to hunt either!

Grey Thunder: Either we eat the babies or the village starves to death!

Billowing Smoke: Hmmmmmmmmmmm! *(Sniffs the air. Pulls the earth tied in leaves from around his neck and sniffs it.)* Hmmmmm. *(Walks to the east sniffs the air. Walks to the west sniffs the air does the same to the north and south).* Kanima nearby....

Growling Tiger: *We* here trying to fend off starvation and *you* searching for *Kanima*?!!

Billowing Smoke: *Gives him as hard look and sniffs again.)*

Eagle Head: Same thing I am saying! This damn Piaiman is no good!!! **(Stalks off into the forest.)**

Growling Tiger follows him.

The other men finish their packing and Exit to the village.

Green Fern, Gentle Breeze and Waking Sun emerge from the bushes where they have been watching the men on the beach.

Gentle Breeze: Green Fern, why are we always hiding in the bush?

Waking Sun: We're girls!

Green Fern: So?

Waking Sun: Our place is in the village. Where we're safe. The world is dangerous. So *that*!

Green Fern: The world is exciting!

Gentle Breeze: And dangerous!

Green Fern: More exciting than dangerous !

Waking Sun: You just jealous that your brother Little Snake gets to spend all his time with your father and grandfather!

Green Fern: I am not jealous! But why should he learn to shoot wild hogs and I can't?

Gentle Breeze: Ekkkkkkk! Who wants to kill hogs for fun?! Nasty!

Fern: Not too nasty to eat though!

Waking Sun: Look! Lets go back ok. It's getting dark and we are going to get into trouble for following crazy-head Fern out here!

Green Fern: But seriously...what would happen if all the men in this village disappeared one day?

Gentle Breeze: That would never happen!

Green Fern: Why?!

Gentle Breeze: They stronger than us!

Green Fern: Says who?!

Waking Sun: Girl! Don't be stupid! Look at all the things they can do and we can't. Build canoe, shoot Tiger, lift it up, bring it home....

Green Fern: And who say we can't do that too?

Waking Sun: To Gentle Breeze) Look. Lets go home now ok. *(They begin to walk off.)*

Green Fern: *Follows them)* But just think about it...what would happen if all the men in the village disappeared nuh?

Waking Sun: We would not have a problem Fern. Since they stronger than us, anybody dying the women will die first . So you see, we don't have nothing to worry about! Come hurry!!!

Green Fern: *Sighs)* I didn't say anything about dying. I said disappear....

Gentle Breeze: Die, disappear, who care? Right now I hungry and there is no fish and no hog!

Waking Sun : Well at least there is Tapioca....

Green Fern: Look! I am so tried of eating Cassava!!! Fry cassava, boil cassava, roast cassava, stew cassava...

Waking Sun: Ok! Ok! But at least it will keep us from starving....

Green Fern: Yes. True. *(Passes by Bush Dai-Dai and gives her a hug.)* This is my favorite bush in the whole forest!

Gentle Breeze: Girl you real strange! A favorite *bush* now?!

Green Fern: Yes.

Waking Sun: *Touching the tree.)* So why it so special?

Green Fern: Saved me from Kanima yesterday!

Waking Sun: *Laughing)* Kanima!? Girl *you* could make up tales!!!!

Green Fern: It's true!

Gentle Breeze: But there has been no Kanima here for years!

Green Fern: There is one here! I am telling you. And you heard my grandfather Billowing Smoke just now. He confirmed it!

Waking Sun: Ok. But you know if you really meet up Kanima there is *nothing* that could save you.

Fern: *This* bush saved me, ok!!

Gentle Breeze: How?

172

Green Fern: By reasoning with the Kanima…

Waking Sun: Laughing) Reasoning? Now the bush could *reason*?

Gentle Breeze and Waking Sun laugh.

Green Fern storms off.

Gentle Breeze and Waking Sun: *Continue to laugh)* Fern! Where you going?! Aren't you afraid that Kanima will get you?!

Green Fern: *Mutters)* Idiots!

Gentle Breeze: Ok. Green Fern. Look we're sorry. Just come on back with us ok...

Green Fern: *Calling)* Find your own way!

Waking Sun: We can't find it in the dark! Come on!!

Green Fern: Too bad!

Enter Growling Tiger.

Growling Tiger: Hello ladies!!

Waking Sun: Hello, Uncle.

Gentle Breeze: Hello...

Growling Tiger: You girls lost I suppose?

Gentle Breeze: No...not really....

Waking Sun: Yes! Yes uncle, we are!

Growling Tiger: You shouldn't be wandering around the forest like this....

Gentle Breeze: It was Green Fern....

Growling Tiger: Green Fern? Was she with you?

Gentle Breeze: Yes. But she went off just now.

Growling Tiger: Which way did she go?

Gentle Breeze and Waking Sun point in the direction that Green Fern went.)

Growling Tiger: Ok. You wait right here, I will get her and bring her back.

Gentle Breeze: Can't we accompany you uncle?

Growling Tiger: No! You will slow me down!

Waking Sun: But it's dark here!

Growling Tiger: Look! Stop whining and stay put! *(Hurries away sniffing the air.)*

As he passes Bush Dai - Dai she puts out her foot and trips him. He manifests as Kanaima

Dai: Where you off to now?

Kanima: I looking for a lost child...

Dai: *Whistles three times.)* I don't have to look. I have eyes and ears all over this forest.

Kanima: Look. I have no time....

Dai: *Listening)* Aha. Aha. *(Kanima)* Well, you say you have to search. Well go search....

Kanima hurries on.

Lights Fade to Black.

Scene 3

The next day. The Village. Twilight. Lights up to with the sounds of stones and percussion, Tom-Tom drums in a slow staccato beat. This music is held under for the entire scene. There is a fire and the villagers are sitting in a wide circle around it. Some of the women are moaning in grief.

Billowing Smoke: *Inhales deeply from a ceremonial pipe and puffs smoke high into the air.)*

The moaning women quiet down and pay rapt attention.

Billowing Smoke takes another pull from the pipe. Inhales and again exhales a puff of smoke high into the air. He signals with his hands to the drum beaters.

The drum beaters pick up the beat a little and drum a little louder.

Billowing Smoke inhales a third time from the pipe and this time as he exhales the smoke he rises and begins a slow twirling dance all around the fire.

One by one the men join him and then the boys join in.

The women rise and keep time maintaining the circle all the while but they never join the dance with the men.

Billowing Smoke begins to shake. Gives out a loud shriek and suddenly stops dancing. The drummers slow down their beat and drop the volume. The women sit down again. The men and boys also sit again.

Billowing Smoke: Makoniama. The great spirit has spoken. Kanima is once again among us.
His twin of treachery and evil has come to this place again! (*Turns to the villagers*) You are here! I know that you are here! Among us! One of us!!! (*He walks over to Red Dust, grabs his hair and looks into his eyes*) Red Dust! My own blood! Is it you?

Red Dust: Noooooooo! I could never do harm to my own people!

Billowing Smoke: *Releases him and walks over to Eagle Head*) Eagle Head! My nephew! Speak! Are you the man-beast among us?!

Eagle Head: I live in the spirit of Makonaima!

Billowing Smoke: *Releases him and crosses to Terrible Moon*) Moon, son of my dear friend Purple Mist, are you the one bringing this confusion among us?!

Terrible Moon: I am human, in deed and in spirit. There is no animal in me. Or will there ever be!

Billowing Smoke: *Releases him and crosses to Growling Tiger*) Growling Tiger, you? Can it be you?

Growling Tiger: No. I say no.

Billowing Smoke: I expect no truth from Kanima. That would be like expecting wine from a coconut tree. But the great spirit has spoken and I heard him say

175

Kanima ....his evil twin is here!

Growling Tiger: Maybe you heard him wrong old man! Maybe it's a warning that he is *coming*.

Red Dust: Maybe you heard him right! Remember one of us is still missing....

Eagle Head: Yes! Grey Thunder has not yet returned...

Red Dust: Yes! Perhaps it is he !

Growling Tiger: Yes! I say we go hunt him ! Hunt him! Now!

Green Fern: *Hidden in the bushes)* No!!!

All the villagers freeze.

Billowing Smoke: (*Advancing slowly towards the voice)*Who is that?

Green Fern: It..it is just the bush.

Billowing Smoke: (*Advances some more)* Does the bush have a name?

Green Fern: No. But the bush has eyes. Everywhere.

Billowing Smoke:(*Almost to the bush)* And what did the bush with the million eyes see?

Green Fern: Kanima!

Billowing Smoke: *Pulls back the bush to reveal Green Fern hidden there).* Fern!

Green Fern: *Points to Growling Tiger)* It's him ! Kanima! It's him!'

Growling Tiger: This child should be in bed!

Red Dust: Fern! Do you know what you are saying?

Growling Tiger: She has been drinking the Piwari for sure!

Billowing Smoke: *Motions for them to be quiet)* Come Green Fern. Sit down.

Green Fern: *Sits.)*

Billowing Smoke: What are you doing up at this time of night?

Green Fern: I...I wanted to watch....

Eagle Head: It's not meant for young girls!

Green Fern: I just wanted to see! Why is everything such a secret from us? All I wanted was to see the face of Makoniama when he came to Billowing Smoke!

Billowing Smoke: Ah! Little one. Be calm...

Green Fern: But I saw him and I heard him....!

A loud exclamation goes up from the women.

Yellow Morning: *Gets up from the group, grabs Green Fern and tries to drag her off to the benab*). Green Fern! Stop this lying at once! How could you embarrass us in this way?!

Green Fern: But I saw him! I saw him Mama!

Growling Tiger: You are going to let this impertinent child make such serious accusations against me without some punishment?!

Billowing Smoke: She is just a child!

Growling Tiger: She is a liar!

Green Fern: I am not! It is you! You tried to kill me! And you killed Grey Thunder!

Growling Tiger roars in rage and changes into Kanima form. He pounces on Green Fern.
Billowing Smoke jumps in front of her and receives the blow instead. He falls to the ground.

Red Dust: It's true! It *is* you!

Growling Tiger Growls angrily again. Crashes through the bushes and disappears. A few of the village men chase after him.

Green Fern: Grandpa! Grandpa! Get up! He's getting away!

Billowing Smoke: Ay ... Makoniama. I....I... won't get up this time. No human can withstand the strike of Kanima. (*Motions to Green Fern.*)

Green Fern *kneels beside him.*

Billowing Smoke: *Puts his hand on her head)* You saw him?

Green Fern nods.

Billowing Smoke motions to Brown Sapling.

Brown Sapling brings his ceremonial pipe and fishing rod. She hands the pipe to him.

Yellow Morning motions to Little Snake to go to his grandfather.

Little Snake hesitates. Yellow Morning rises and pushes hi m forward.

Billowing Smoke: *Looks up, sees him)* Grandson....

Little Snake: Yes! Grandfather Billowing Smoke?

Billowing Smoke: You saw Kanima?

Little Snake: *Nods No.)*

Billowing Smoke closes his eyes.

Green Fern: Grandpa!

Billowing Smoke: Ay....Makoniama. I am coming. I pray for a moment more...to finish this......
(Hands the pipe to Little Snake) It has belonged to the men in our family for generations. By taking this from me now, you agree to live the life of the Piaiman and to serve the Great Spirit Makoniama.

Little Snake *Hesitates.*

Yellow Morning *nudges him.*

Little Snake takes the Pipe and takes a pull. He blows the smoke into his sister Green Fern's face. She begins to cough.

Billowing Smoke *puts his shaking hands on Green Fern's head)* You are a special girl. You will make someone a good wife one day. (*Coughs*) Be Good. (*Motions to Brown Sapling to pass the rod.)*

Brown Sapling *passes the rod to Billowing Smoke.)*

Billowing Smoke attempts to lift it but it falls from his lifeless hands. He dies.

Both Green Fern and Little Snake both reach for the rod.

Little Snake: It is mine. *You* should not even *be* here!

Green Fern: I am his grandchild too! I have Piaiman blood too!

Yellow Morning: Green Fern! Billowing Smoke left them to *him*. They are tools. Not playthings!

Brown Sapling kneels beside Billowing Smoke.

The Drummers pick up a mournful rhythm and the women and remaining boys and men begin to chant.

Little Snake takes another puff of the ceremonial pipe and puffs smoke high into the air. Slowly and unsteadily he begins the Piaiman's twirling dance.

Green Fern *watches despondently.*

Lights Fade to Black.

Scene 4

A few days later in the village. Green Fern is trying to get the other girls in the village to go for a swim with her.

Waking Sun: No! Kanima in the bush!

Green Fern: But we won't be going through the bush. I know a clear path straight to the water.

Gentle Breeze: I am too weak. I am too hungry.

Waking Sun: Me too!

Green Fern: Then we could catch some fish!

Waking Sun: Fish? When last you see a fish in these waters girl? You real mad. Just like my mother said!

Gentle Breeze: I am not going anywhere with you anymore. My father said you will lead me astray!

179

Green Fern: Me? What did I do?!

Waking Sun: You trying to be a boy!

Green Fern: No. I am not!

Gentle Breeze: Yes you are! Plus you embarrassed all the women at the ceremony!

Green Fern: No! I just don't want to stay locked up in a house all day working with *Tibiceri*!

Gentle Breeze: You see! Same thing I said!

Green Fern: No! It's not the same thing. I just want to try some different things....

Waking Sun: Why?!

Green Fern: Don't know....You know. Its just something inside. A lot of things that want to just burst out that have no place in a benab!

Waking Sun: You sounding real crazy!

Gentle Breeze: You should get a boyfriend.

Waking Sun: *Giggling*) I like Little Snake.

Green Fern: I like Shaking Arrow....

Waking Sun: My brother?! Really!

Green Fern: You mean you actually *like* a boy?

Waking Sun: Maybe you *really* are a girl after all!

Green Fern: Of course I am a girl. I just don't think that should stop me from doing anything I want .

Waking Sun: Fern. You and I are same age. We grow up together like orchids in a Saman tree. We learn that there are things for boys and things for girls. Nobody don't have any problem with that. So why *you* have to be different?!

Green Fern: Maybe people want to talk about their feelings but they're sacred....

Gentle Breeze: And you not? You don't *care* what people say about you?

Green Fern: Yes. But what I fear more is not to know what I can know.

Waking Sun: Little Snake is all I need to know!

Green Fern: I wasn't talking about *that*!

Waking Sun: Well what else is there!?

Green Fern: So you *sure* you don't want to go for a swim?

Gentle Breeze: You *not* going alone?!

Green Fern: If I have to....

Waking Sun: No! I absolutely say no! Fern it is too dangerous out there.

Green Fern: Ok. See you later.

Gentle Breeze: *Grabbing on to her arm)* Please Fern! Don't go. Please don't go....

Green Fern: It's not far. You all could see me from here just in case anything happens! (*Walks off in the direction of the river.)*

Gentle Breeze: Gosh. ...Gosh...Gosh!

Waking Sun: What's wrong?

Gentle Breeze: Ohhhhhhh! I don't know. She worries me so!

Waking Sun: Yes. I know.

Gentle Breeze: She has me thinking you know. Gosh-gosh.

Waking Sun: About what?

Gentle Breeze: Suppose she is right? About the things she is saying? Suppose us girls could be just as independent and brave as the boys? Look how brave she is!

Waking Sun: She is not brave. She is nuts! Come lets go hunt for something to eat. This hunger is unbearable!

They exit towards the huts.

Green Fern re-enters tiptoeing towards a mat where Little Snake is asleep. *The Fishing rod is propped up against a tree as Little Snake snores. Green Fern looks furtively around and then takes the rod.* **As she takes the rod Brown Sapling enters carrying a basket of cassava.** *Green Fern sees her an is about to replace the rod but Brown Sapling smiles and waves her on her way. Green Fern takes the rod and heads towards the river.* **Brown Sapling chuckles to herself and returns to the hut.**

Green Fern makes her way to the waters edge followed by Bush Dai- Dai. She takes the rod and places it gently in a canoe. She unties the canoe and pushes it out to the water. With great effort she gets it into the river. She climbs into it and rows out to the middle of the water. As she rows, she begins to sing to the fish:

Green Fern: *Ahhhhhhhh! Ahhhhhhh! My lovely fish. Fish , Fish beautiful fish Arapaima, Carass and Horrie, Lukanini and Banga Mary Ahhhhhhhh! Ahhhhhhh! My lovely fish. Show your self in all your beauty From the river deep where you're hiding, to the water's top where I'm riding!*

Green Fern *tosses her line.*

Bush Dai-Dai *watches from a rock on the land and chuckles to herself.*

Green Fern *pulls in the line. It is empty. She continues to sing and toss her line but after three tries there is still no fish.*

Bush Dai-Dai: *Walks to the waters edge.*) Helloooo! Is *time* for some of you to come up now! You hiding down there for months and I helping you. But fish can't live forever and man can't live forever without fish. Let the young ones stay down and the pregnant mamie-Fish stay safe, but let the old one come now and those who dying soon. Come up I say! Come now! All of life is sacrifice! Give yourself to the young girl's rod 'cause she going to give to the human's so much more than fish in just a few hours time! Lukanani, full up her boat. Come!

Green Fern tosses her line again and this time she gets a fish. This she does over and over until she gets several fish. Some she keeps others she gently releases back into the water.

Bush Dai -Dai: Yes. At least the village will eat for a few days and they will see that a daughter can provide as well as a son. And they will stop laughing at my Green Fern!

Green Fern rows the boat to shore humming a happy song. She begins to unload her fish and strings them all together on a pole for ease of carriage.

182

Enter Little Snake.

Green Fern: Little Snake! Little Snake look! (*Happily shows him the fish.*)

Little Snake: *Looks at the fish in disbelief)* You took my rod?!!

Green Fern: Yes! But look ! The village can eat now!

Little Snake: You *stole* my belongings!

Green Fern: I borrowed it! Oh ! Don't be mad. I found the fish!

Little Snake: Show me!

Green Fern: *Pointing to the place in the river.)*

Little Snake: Liar! I fished there yesterday. It was bare!

Green Fern: That is the place. I swear!

Little Snake: *Pushing the Canoe out to the water)* Well lets see you do it again!

Green Fern: But what does it matter? We have enough for a whole week already!

Little Snake: You stole my rod. The *least* you can do is show me where to fish!

Green Fern: *Sighs. Lays her fish down on the bank)* Ok. I'll show you. (*Climbs into the boat.*)

Little Snake Pushes the boat out as far as possible then takes the oars and runs off leaving Green Fern stranded in the middle of the water.

Green Fern: Little Snake. Brother! What are you doing?

Little Snake: See you later, little sister! (*Takes up the fish on the shore and heads off.*)

Green Fern: But how will I get out of here? It's too deep and the water is full of Pirai!

Little Snake: Someone will rescue you! Just stay put for a few hours!

Green Fern: Bother! Please don't leave me here!

Little Snake Exits to the Village carrying the Fish.

Green Fern: Brother! Brother! Help! Somebody!

Enter Kanima on top of the second largest mountain.
He hears Green Fern's cries. Looks in her direction and laughs evilly.

Black Out.

Scene 5

Lights up on the village that same night. There is a great big fire and jubilation. Laughter and music is heard as well as singing. There is a spit across the fire upon which fish is roasting. The men of the village bring in the ceremonial stool.

Enter Little Snake.

Everyone except Brown Sapling cheer, hoot and applaud Little Snake's entrance.

Yellow Morning detaches herself from the crowd and brings her son to the ceremonial stool.

Little Snake sits.

Yellow Morning *sits upon the ground next to him. She beckons to Brown Sapling.*

Brown Sapling turns away and ignores Yellow Morning.

Red Dust: My son has brought us prosperity!

The villagers applaud.

Red Dust: Almost two months since we have not seen a fish in this village.

Yellow Morning: We were starving!

Red Dust: My son has brought us fish!

Villagers applaud again.

184

Red Dust: His grandfather has blessed him from beyond. It is clear that Makoniama himself has smiled upon him.

Villagers applaud again.

Red Dust: *Standing behind Little Snake's stool)* I am proud to be the father of such a wonderful son!

Villagers applaud again.

Little Snake motions for them to be silent.

The villagers fall silent.

Little Snake: I have only three things to say. Eat, drink and be merry! (*Pulls the spit off the fire and passes it around as others put another spit with more fish to roast. He offers his father, then is mother. They both partake. He offers Brown Sapling. She refuses. Little Snake tries to persuade her but she refuses him. He gives her a deep dark look and then offers the fish to Waking Sun.*)

Waking Sun takes the fish and hands a piece to Gentle Breeze.

Gentle Breeze: Have you seen Fern all night?

Waking Sun: No....

Gentle Breeze: Do you think she is ok?

Waking Sun: Of course! She can take care of herself.

Gentle Breeze: Still. She has never stayed out this late all by herself....

Waking Sun: Well she choose a wrong night to go on her travels. Look what she is missing out! (*Laughs.*)

Breeze: I think something is wrong. I can feel a frown upon the night....

Waking Sun: Yes! Cause you're putting it there! Don't be a spoil sport Breeze! Not tonight! (*Breaks a piece of her fish and gives it to Breeze*) Here take another piece. Nothing like a nice full belly to help you forget things!

Breeze refuses the fish and wanders off.

Waking Sun shrugs and crosses to Little Snake.

185

The lights on the village dim.

Spotlight on Green Fern in the canoe. The music from the village can still be heard low.

Bush Dai-Dai stands as close as possible to the waters edge.

Dai: Blow gentle wind and blow warm as night wind can blow. The child is out there with no cover to protect her.

Kanima: The wind is not your servant Dai-Dai. Blow wind-blow! Blow deep and blow strong! Stir the river. Show your might! Tonight!

Dai: Water be steady. Don't rock her boat. Keep her safely till the sunlight comes!

Kanima: Churn river! Twist your guts and spew your anger! What right has man to squat their canoes on your face? To toss their refuse into your stillness?! Overthrow the damn boat!

Dai: If the river rocks the boat. Fish ! You all hold it steady!

Kanima: If the fish fight against the current, rapids drown them! *(Laughs.)*

Green Fern: *Calling out)* Help! Somebody help me!

Dai: Stay calm child. The morning will soon come.

Kanima Laughs again.

Green Fern: All that merriment in the village! Nobody will hear me !

Dai: Wait. Tomorrow soon coming.

Green Fern: It's not fair! He stole my fish and on top of everything they treating him as if he is a hero! Is *my* fish! *I* catch the fish! They should be celebrating *me*!

Dai: Fish love you child. I will give you more! And anything that you want.

Green Fern: And now I hungry! They eating my fish and I soooooooo hungry!

Dai: Drink river water and stay easy. Tomorrow you will feast. I promise.

Kanima: Tomorrow?! She ain't making it past midnight! Dai-Dai. I told you I wouldn't give up! I told you!

Green Fern: Look. This water looking very calm all of a sudden. And the wind so gentle. You know, I sure I can swim ashore now. It not so far....

Dai: What?!

Kanima Laughs.

Green Fern: *Dips her hands into the water)* Water nice and warm too! (*Jumps into the river.*)

Dai: No! Fern! Makoniama ! Do something! She going to drown!

Kanima: Yes! Drown the little nosy wretch! Let she drown!

Green Fern: Oh! Oh!

Kanima: Churn river! Churn!

Dai: Don't listen to him! This is an innocent child!

Kanima: She is an upstart! An aberration ! She alone could see me!

Green Fern: Help! Some....body....help...I'm going down....

Kanima: *Laughs)* Yes. You are going down!

Dai: *Besides herself)* Fish, Snake, Turtle, Manatee you all do something!

Fern: *Feebly)* He—lp. (*Disappears under the water.*)

Kanima :*Jumping down from his perch in front of Dai-Dai)* She gone. You lose. I tell you not to cross me! (*Hits Dai-Dai a lash and sends her flying as he disappears.*)

The wind begins to howl and a loud flash of lightening is seen.

Dai: *Pulls herself together and weeps at the waters edge)* Ow Green Fern. My daughter. They kill you!
I couldn't save you this time! And all them in the village eating and drinking off the fat of your love while you sinking to the river bank with black water in your lungs. Owwwww! Fern!

Thunder and flashing lightening again.

Dai: *Eyes cast to the sky*) What *you* come for now?! *You* can't do nothing now!

Thunder again and light at the top of the highest mountain. A beautiful woman appears in the light.

Makoniama: Stop your grieving Dai-Dai. The girl will live.

Dai: You going to bring Green Fern back?

Makoniama: She will be truly one of us now Dai-Dai.

Dai: How that could be?

Makoniama: I am great spirit and I say it will be. Go to the water and look.

Dai looks at the river.

Green Fern emerges from the water up to her waist.

Dai: Fern! Its you? Come out of the water let me touch you?

Green Fern swims up to the waters edge and then struggles on to the beach for now she has the tail of a fish.

Dai: Is that what you do? Turn she into a fish?!

Makoniama: You see fish. I see goddess. She will have powers of life and death over all men who travel this river from this day on. (*To Green Fern)* I return to you, what they stole from you. Use it wisely Fair maid.

Green Fern nods and disappears back into the water.

Kanaima enters. *Approaches the village.*

There is a huge crack of lightening and thunder.

Dead Blackout.

The End.

Glossary and Notes for A Fairmaid's Tale

Amerindians – The general name used to describe the native peoples of Guyana who make up about 2% of the country's present population. They are however a diverse people including such groups as Caribs, Akowaios, Wai-wai, Wapishanas, Warraus, Arawaks and Patimonas.

Arapaima – Arguably the largest fresh water fish in the world. It is found in the interior rivers of the Guianas and can grow to lengths of about six feet. It is an Amerindian staple and the national fish of Guyana.

Banga Mary – A type of fish.

Benab – A circular bamboo structure with a thatched roof used as by Amerindians as their homes.

Casareep – Special preservative made by Guyanese Amerindian's from the juice of Cassava. It is brown in color and has the look and consistency of molasses. It is used as the base for a Pepperpot which is a meaty stew that Guyanese Amerindians make.

Cassava – This is a ground provision or root crop also known as Yucca yams.

Dai –Dai / Bush Dai-Dai – Amerindian spirit of the forests who protects the gold and diamond and treasures of nature. Has the appearance of a bush or tree.

Kanima – The evil, negative force in Amerindian mythology. He is the twin of Makonaima who can assume human and any animal form. In this play he is Growling Tiger in his human form and a Tiger in his mythical form. As such both Kanima and Growling Tiger are aspects of a single character.

Lukananee – Type of fresh water fish.

Mako /Makonaima – The great spirit. The creative, good and benevolent twin of Amerindian mythology.

Piaiman /Piaiwoman - Amerindian spiritual leader or medicine man. Can be male or female but is usually male.

Pirana – Man eating fish.

Piwari – A particularly potent Amerindian alcoholic drink made from the fermented juice of the Cassava.

Tibiceri – A particularly strong palm found in the interior of Guyana. It has a variety of uses such as thatching for the roofs of benabs, weaving for mats, baskets, hats and some articles of clothing.

FURTHER READING

Much of the research for this book was taken from unpublished manuscripts and from oral interviews I conducted. However the following are some books that may enrich your perspective on these subjects.

Warner - Lewis, Maureen. *Guineas Other Suns.* The Majority Press, Dover. MA. 1991.

Nagamotoo, Moses. *Henderee's Cure*. Peepal Tree Press, London. 2000.

Khemraj, Harischarndra , *Cosmic Dance*. Peepal Tree Press. London. 1994.

Singh, Roopnandan. *Wild Mamie*. Roopnandan Singh Publications. Georgetown. 1996.

Seymour, A. J . *A Dictionary of Guyanese Folklore*. Guyana History and Arts Council. Georgetown. 1975.

Persaud, Satnarine – Names of Some Folk Spirits in Guyana in *Rickford*, J (Ed). *A Festival of Guyanese Words*. University of Guyana. Georgetown. 1978.

Parmasad, Kenneth Vidia. *Salt and Roti*. Sankh Publications. Trinidad. 1986.

Lannoy, Richard. *The Speaking Tree*. Oxford University Press. London. 1971.

Braithwaithe, Barrington. *The Silk Cotton Tree*. Spectrum Creative Productions. Georgetown. 1999.

CPSIA information can be obtained
at www.ICGtesting.com
Printed in the USA
FSHW011942290120
66639FS